Orlando

by Emma Stanford

Emma Stanford has written books and articles on Florida, California, the Caribbean, Hawaii, France and Spain, as well as Mediterranean port guides for the US navy. She has also contributed to guides published by the BTA, American Express and Fodor.

GW00497277

AA Publishing

Above: *live at Gatorworld*

Written by Emma Stanford

First published 1998
Reprinted June and October 1999
Reprinted April 2000
Revised second edition 2001
Reprinted June 2001
Reprinted March, June and October 2002
Reprinted 2004. Information verified and updated
Reprinted April 2004. Reprinted May 2004 and Aug 2004

© Automobile Association Developments Limited 1998, 2001

Published by AA Publishing, a trading name of Automobile Association Developments Limited, whose registered office is Millstream, Maidenhead Road, Windsor, SL4 5GD Registered number 1878835.

A02333

Colour separation: BTB Digital Imaging Ltd, Whitchurch, Hampshire
Printed and bound in Italy by Printers Trento S.r.l.

Find out more about AA Publishing and the wide range of travel publications and services the AA provides by visiting our website at www.theAA.com

Contents

About this Book

This book is divided into five sections to cover the most important aspects of your visit to Orlando.

Viewing Orlando pages 5–14

An introduction to Orlando by the author.

Orlando's Features
Essence of Orlando
The Shaping of Orlando
Peace and Quiet
Orlando's Famous

Top Ten pages 15–26

The author's choice of the Top Ten places to see in and around Orlando, each with practical information.

What to See pages 27–90

The three main areas in and around Orlando, each with its own brief introduction and an alphabetical listing of the main attractions.

Practical information
Snippets of 'Did You Know…' information
5 suggested tours
2 features

Where To... pages 91–116

Detailed listings of the best places to eat, stay, shop, take the children and be entertained.

Practical Matters pages 117–24

A highly visual section containing essential travel information.

Maps

All map references are to the individual maps found in the What to See section of this guide.

For example, Busch Gardens has the reference ➕ 46A1 – indicating the page on which the map is located and the grid square in which the attraction is to be found. A list of the maps that have been used in this travel guide can be found in the index.

Prices

Where appropriate, an indication of the cost of an establishment is given by **£** signs:

£££ denotes higher prices, **££** denotes average prices, while **£** denotes lower charges.

Star Ratings

Most of the places described in this book have been given a separate rating:

✪✪✪ Do not miss
✪✪ Highly recommended
✪ Worth seeing

Viewing
Orlando

Above: *face-painting
at Lake Eola Park*
Right: *Southern
belle, Cypress
Gardens*

Emma Stanford's Orlando

Dolphins working out at SeaWorld Orlando

Getting Around

Short-stay visitors can tackle Orlando without a car, though public transport is pretty sketchy. Most hotels offer free shuttles to Walt Disney World, and Orlando's International Drive resort area has the cheap and efficient I-Ride trolley bus (7AM–midnight, stopping every two blocks between SeaWorld Orlando and Belz Factory Outlet mall). For longer stays, independent transport is a worthwhile investment, opening up a host of alternative day trips to the Gulf coast or Atlantic beaches, state parks and other Central Florida attractions.

Orlando really is the town that Mickey Mouse built. A former cattle ranchers' watering hole and citrus depot in dusty Central Florida, the quiet country town boomed after the opening of the first Walt Disney World theme park, Magic Kingdom, in 1971. Today, Orlando is firmly established as one of the world's top holiday destinations.

More than 38 million visitors pour into Orlando every year; over the past quarter century, over 500 million have visited Walt Disney World Resort. The sheer volume of interest in Orlando has meant that the city has grown fast – often too fast for developers to concern themselves with the niceties of landscaping or public transport – and the main tourist areas have spread out well beyond Orlando itself. Many visitors to Walt Disney World Resort, a 30-minute drive south of International Drive, choose to stay in the neighbouring town of Kissimmee. However, what Orlando may lack in aesthetic urban planning it more than makes up for in thrills, spills and Disney magic. This is theme park heaven, boasting state-of-the-art rides, family entertainment and fantasy on tap. Add gratifyingly high standards of service and you have a holiday destination that could teach the rest of the world a thing or two.

Orlando's Features

Distances
• Distance from Miami: 236 miles
• Distance from New York: 944 miles
• Distance from Los Angeles: 2,203 miles
• Distance from London: 4,336 miles

Size
• Population: 180,500 (City of Orlando); 1.6 million (Greater Orlando)
• Population density: 4,000 people per square mile
• Annual visitors: 43 million

Geography
• Latitude: N 28° 32'
• Longitude: W 81° 22'
• Height above sea level: 70 feet

Climate
• Warmest months: July–August (high 92°F, low 73°F)
• Coolest month: January (high 72°F, low 49°F)
• Wettest month: July (7.8 inches of rain)
• Driest months: November–December (1.8 inches of rain)

Facilities
• Hotel rooms: 105,000
• Restaurants: 4,300-plus
• Visitor attractions: 95
• Golf courses: 150-plus
• Tennis courts: 800
• Watersports: 300-plus inland lakes, springs and rivers for fishing, swimming and boating; an hour's drive from the Atlantic and Gulf coasts
• Spectator sports: basketball (Orlando Magic and Women's NBA team, Orlando Miracle); baseball (Orlando Rays and spring training visitors, the Atlanta Braves and Houston Astros); American football (Orlando Predators)
• Retail shopping space: 50 million square feet
• Transport: Orlando International Airport is the 15th busiest in the US (24th in the world), with around 900 flights daily serving more than 100 cities worldwide.

Top: *the Orlando skyline*
Above: *catching the surf on the Atlantic coast*

As You Like It
There are two versions of how Orlando came to be named. One credits pioneer settler and local big-wig, Judge V D Speer, with having named the town after a character in his favourite Shakespeare play, *As You Like It*. The other is that the town was named after Orlando Reeves, a US soldier killed by an Indian arrow in 1835 while raising the alarm to save his company, in what is now downtown Orlando's Lake Eola Park.

7

Essence of Orlando

Below: *Woody Woodpecker, a favourite with younger guests*
Bottom: *fun on the rapids at Busch Gardens*

The essence of Orlando is entertainment. From the tips of Disney-MGM Studios' Earffel Tower down to the sandy bunkers of more than 100 golf courses, Orlando is a full-on, year-round crowd pleaser. Visitors can share their breakfast muffins with Goofy and the gang, lunch in Splendid China, get whisked aboard a Magic Carpet at the Arabian Nights dinner theatre and never really set foot in Florida. But this would be a mistake. Beyond the man-made wonders, Central Florida offers sparkling lakes, citrus groves, lovely gardens and a rich and varied wildlife showcased in relaxing state parks.

THE **10** ESSENTIALS

*If you only have a short time to visit Orlando,
or would like to get a really complete picture of the
region, here are the essentials:*

• **Magic Kingdom:** the 'must see' classic Disney park (➤ 84–7).
• **T2:3-D:** one of the hottest hi-tech theme park thrills to arrive in recent times, Universal Studios' Terminator 2 'virtual adventure' has become a classic (➤ 40).
• **Manatees**, or sea cows, are the endangered gentle giants of Florida's waterways. If you cannot get to see them in the wild (➤ 51), do not miss SeaWorld's Manatees: The Last Generation? (➤ 36).
• **Do the birdwalk**, a little-known secret: the Gatorland marsh boardwalk is one of the best birdwatching spots in the region (➤ 32).
• **Blooming marvellous:** for local horticultural colour, enjoy the formal delights of the Harry P. Leu Gardens (➤ 33), or the woodland trails of Bok Tower

Gardens (➤ 47).
• **Silver Spurs:** cattle ranchers first settled the area in the 1840s and Kissimmee celebrates its origins with the biannual Silver Spurs Rodeo (➤ 60).
• **Drink up!** Florida produces around 75 per cent of the nation's citrus crop, so be sure to sample fresh local juices.
• **Shop 'til you drop:** the top end of Orlando's International Drive has turned into a magnet for bargain-hunters, with factory outlet stores galore (➤ 105).
• **Look into the future:** forget sci-fi for a moment and head 'Behind the Seeds' at Disney's Epcot Center for a fascinating look at the future of agriculture (➤ 81).

Above: *fresh Florida oranges*
Below: *enjoying the show at Fort Liberty*

• **Doing dinner** can be quite an event in Orlando. A host of popular dinner theatres offers themed evenings from Medieval Times to 1930s-style Capone's (➤ 113).

The Shaping of Orlando

Spanish explorer Juan Ponce de León found Florida while looking for the fountain of youth

1513
Spanish explorer Juan Ponce de León discovers Florida.

1565
Pedro Menéndez de Avilés, Captain General of the Spanish treasure fleets, founds St Augustine on the Atlantic coast, the oldest continuously inhabited European settlement in the US.

1763–83
The British occupy Florida for 20 years before it is returned to Spain under the Second Treaty of Paris.

1817–18
Tensions between the incoming white settlers and native American Seminole Indians spark the First Seminole War.

1819
Spain relinquishes Florida to the US in settlement of a $5 million debt.

1835–42
Second Seminole War. Fort Gatlin established close to present-day Orlando c 1837.

1842
The US army escorts 3,000 Seminole Indians on the 'Trail of Tears' to exile on reservations west of the Mississippi. Settlers move into Central Florida.

1843
Cattleman pioneer Aaron Jernigan arrives from Georgia, and constructs a stockade on the shores of Lake Holden. The early settlement in the vicinity of Fort Gatlin is named Jernigan in 1850.

1845
Florida achieves statehood.

1857
Jernigan is renamed Orlando (see panel on ► 7). Local settlers make their living from cattle-ranching and cotton.

1861
Florida is the third state to secede from the Union and join the Confederacy. Start of the Civil War (1861–5).

1865
WH Holden plants Orlando's first

commercial citrus plantation on his 100-acre property. At first the fruit has to be hauled overland to Sanford and then carried by boat to markets in Charleston, South Carolina.

1875
The City of Orlando (all 2 square miles of it), county seat of Orange County, is officially incorporated by a vote of 22 men from the total population of 85.

1880
Henry Plant's South Florida Railroad links Kissimmee/Orlando to Tampa on the Gulf coast.

1890s
English settlers buy up land around Orlando for around $1 an acre and plant citrus.

1894–5
The Great Freeze devastates Central Florida's citrus groves. Faced with ruin, the English settlers are rumoured to have consoled themselves by playing cricket. Meanwhile, orange-grower John B Steinmetz converts his packing house into a skating rink with picnic facilities, a toboggan slide and a bath house, creating Orlando's first visitor attraction.

1922
First cargo planes land at Orlando, followed by passengers in 1928.

1929
Mediterranean fruit fly attacks citrus orchards in the Orlando area. The National Guard are called out to enforce quarantine regulations and spray the infected crop, and the threat is eradicated within a year.

1956
The Glenn L Martin Company of Baltimore (now Lockheed Martin) annouces plans to build a missile factory in Orange County, giving a considerable boost to the local economy, together with the proximity of the new Cape Canaveral aerospace complex.

1965
Walt Disney announces his plans for Walt Disney World.

1971
The first phase of Walt Disney World, Magic Kingdom, opens.

1977
The last orange grove on Orlando's famous Orange Avenue is bulldozed to make way for a shopping centre.

1983
Epcot Center opens.

1989
Disney–MGM Studios opens. The three Walt Disney World theme parks comprise the world's number one tourist destination.

1990
Universal Studios opens.

1998
Walt Disney World opens Disney's Animal Kingdom, its fourth full-size theme park.

1999
Universal Studios unveils a second theme park, Islands of Adventure, and a full vacation resort complex.

The space shuttle Discovery *taking off*

Peace & Quiet

Escaping the hustle and bustle of Orlando's theme parks and non-stop fun is not only an attractive idea but essential if you are spending more than a few days in town. Though Central Florida is not renowned for its scenery – undulating citrus groves are the main feature – it is remarkably easy to step back from the concrete jungle and discover pockets of wild, undeveloped natural Florida just around the corner.

Water, Water Everywhere

Below: *taking life easy: there are plenty of boating opportunities in Orlando*
Inset: *the unusual anhinga or 'snakebird'*

There are more than 300 named lakes and dozens of rivers, ponds and springs in the vicinity of Orlando, offering excellent bass-fishing, boating and swimming opportunities. They also act as a magnet for wildlife, particularly waterbirds such as herons, snowy egrets, coots, gallinules and the bizarre-looking anhinga bird, which swims with its body beneath the surface and only its long, thin, snake-like neck protruding.

A boat tour of Lake Tohopekaliga, in Kissimmee, is a great way to get away from it all, and there is a good chance of spotting bald eagles and osprey, as well as more common species. Tours depart from the marina and there are boats and fishing tackle for hire (➤ 61). There are also scenic boat trips on Winter Park's lakes, where wildlife plays second string to expensive lakeshore real estate, but the odd alligator occasionally surfaces to give passengers a thrill for their money (➤ 67).

Nature Trails

Within easy reach of Orlando, there are more than half-a-dozen state parks giving access to unspoilt wilderness, marshland boardwalks and nature trails for wildlife-spotting, as well as canoe runs, fishing lakes and picnic grounds in a natural setting. North of Orlando, the sand pine woods of Ocala National Forest are one of the last refuges of the Florida black bear and home to barred owls and wild turkeys. A 66-mile section of the cross-state Florida National Scenic Trail runs through the forest, and there are numerous shorter trails, while canoe runs such as Juniper

Harry P. Leu Gardens, a wonderful haven of peace in downtown Orlando

Springs are reckoned to be among the best in the state (➤ 62).

For winter visitors to picturesque Blue Spring State Park, on the St John's River, there is the added incentive of spotting a manatee (➤ 51). You could combine a nature walk with a visit to the beach on a day trip to Merritt Island National Wildlife Refuge and the Canaveral National Seashore, in the shadow of the Kennedy Space Center launch pad on the Atlantic Coast (➤ 58).

Glorious Gardens

If nature in the raw does not appeal, there is peace and quiet to be found in a brace of delightful gardens. Just north of downtown, Harry P. Leu Gardens is a tranquil lakeshore spot boasting one of the finest camellia collections in the US (➤ 33). The shady woodlands of Bok Tower Gardens, near Lake Wales, make a soothing escape, where the only sound to disturb the birdsong is the chimes of the famous carillon (➤ 47).

Orlando's Famous

Osceola, champion of the Seminoles, pictured in about 1830

Osceola

A charismatic warrior and the principal native American leader of the Second Seminole War, Osceola (c1803–38) settled near the Peace River south of Orlando in around 1808. Utterly opposed to the forced migration of Seminole Indians to reservations west of the Mississippi, Osceola's hostility towards white settlers and the US government was further inflamed by the kidnap of his wife, Che-cho-ter (Morning Dew), whose trace of Negro blood allowed her white captors to claim she was a fugitive slave. After executing a Miccosukee chief for accepting government money to migrate, Osceola led an attack on Fort King which triggered the outbreak of war in 1835. Public outcry greeted Osceola's unlawful capture while negotiating under a flag of truce in 1837, but he was held in St Augustine and transferred to Fort Moultrie, South Carolina, where he died.

Zora Neale Hurston

Celebrated Black folklorist and writer Zora Neale Hurston (1903–60), was born and raised north of Orlando, in Eatonville, one of the first incorporated Negro towns in the US. Employing the language of the rural Black south, she wrote evocatively of her people. Her mostly widely acclaimed novel, *Their Eyes Were Watching God*, was published in 1937, and an autobiography, *Dust Tracks on a Road*, in 1942. See also ► 69.

Mickey Mouse

Mickey Mouse was born in California in 1928 (► panel). He made his first screen appearance that year in *Steamboat Willie*, and went on to star in more than 100 cartoon movies, including a challenging role as the Sorcerer's Apprentice in *Fantasia* (1940). Mickey and his companion, Minnie, established a base in Florida in 1971 and also have homes in France and Japan.

A Star is Born

As a teenager living in Kansas, the man behind the Mouse, Walter Elias Disney (1901–66), took a correspondence course in cartoon-drawing. When a successful early cartoon character, Oswald the Lucky Rabbit, fell victim to an unscrupulous distributor, Disney returned to the drawing board and created Mortimer Mouse, inspired, so the story goes, by the field mice that used to frequent his old Kansas City studio. The mouse was renamed Mickey by Disney's wife, Lillian. The rest is history.

Top Ten

Above: *whale at SeaWorld Orlando*
Right: *posing at Kennedy Space Center*

1
Busch Gardens

Hold on for a stomach-churning ride

The combination of exotic animals, thrilling roller-coasters, water rides and shows makes this one of Florida's top attractions.

Busch Gardens lies around 75 minutes' drive west of Orlando, in Tampa. Opened in 1959, it is a seasoned crowd-pleaser with pleasantly mature grounds shaded by trees and flowering shrubs. The overall plot is 'Africa', with 10 themed areas such as Nairobi, Timbuktu and the Serengeti Plain; the latter incorporates the interactive Edge of Africa domain, inaugurated in the summer of 1997.

The 335-acre park houses one of the nation's premier zoos. There are more than 2,800 animals from over 300 species wandering the grassland enclosures of the Serengeti Plain, inhabiting the rocks and waterfalls of the Great Ape Domain and featured in other displays such as the Bird Gardens. Busch Gardens plays a significant role in breeding and conserving endangered species and many of the zoo's latest additions are proudly displayed in the Nairobi Animal Nursery.

But animals are by no means all the park has to offer: roller-coaster fans are also in for a big treat. Check out the duelling, double wooden roller-coaster Gwazi and Montu, one of the tallest and longest inverted coasters in the world. The Kumba ride remains among the largest and fastest steel roller-coasters in existence, and assorted water rides provide varying degrees of thrills and spills, plus a chance to cool off in the Florida sunshine.

Small children are particularly well catered-for here. In addition to the animal attractions, there is the interactive Land of the Dragons play area, and colourful ice shows in the Moroccan Palace Theater. Strollers are available for rental in the Morocco district and there is a full baby-changing and nursing area in Land of the Dragons.

See also ➤ 48–50.

Off map 46A1

Busch Boulevard, Tampa (75 miles west of Orlando via I-4 West and I-75 North to Fowler Avenue/Exit 54)

(813) 987 5082 or 1-888 800 5447

Daily 10–6 (extended summer and hols)

Refreshment stops throughout park, plus the full-service Crown Colony Restaurant (Crown Colony) (£–££)

Very good

Very expensive

Check daily schedules for show times

2
Cypress Gardens

Florida's first theme park remains faithful to its botanical origins and is famous for its four annual flower festivals.

Sloping gently down to the shores of Lake Eloise, near Winter Haven, a 45-minute drive south of Orlando, Cypress Gardens was originally laid out in the 1930s along the swampy water's edge, shaded by giant cypress trees. The park has expanded considerably since, covering more than 220 acres, and offers a variety of shows, shopping, dining and animal attractions in addition to the carefully manicured gardens, eye-catching topiary and other horticultural exhibits.

For plant-lovers, the lush Botanical Gardens remain the highlight of a visit. Shaded brick paths meander through dense tropical plantings of heliconias and bromeliads, cascades of brilliantly coloured bougainvillea and forests of bamboo. There are acres of formal gardens, too, and for sheer spectacle it is hard to beat the Spring Flower Festival, November's Mum Festival, featuring more than 3 million chrysanthemum blooms, and the winter holiday Poinsettia Festival.

Flower power aside, Cypress Gardens takes pride in its water-ski revues on the lake, and the 153-foot-high Island in the Sky revolving observatory. At its foot, Southern Crossroads houses snack stops, restaurants and shops.

Other attractions concentrate on the wonders of the natural world, with the Butterfly Conservatory, Gator Gulch and the Nature's Way area featuring animal enclosures and a wooden boardwalk area on the lake. The latest family fun addition is the Wacky Water Park. See also ➤ 52.

46B1

SR540 W, 4 miles east of Winter Haven (off US27, 22 miles south of I-4)

(863) 324 2111 or 1-800 282 2123

Daily 5:30–9 (extended for special events)

Crossroads Restaurant & Terrace (£–££); Cypress BBQ (£); Village Fare Food Court (£); assorted snack and refreshment stops (£)

Very good

Very expensive

Bok Tower Gardens (➤ 47), Lake Wales (➤ 61)

During high season reservations are advised for dinner cruises aboard the *Southern Breeze* paddle-wheel boat

Cypress Gardens, colourful at any time of the year

17

3
Discovery Cove

29B2

6000 Discovery Cove Way (1-4/Exit 71 or 72)

(407) 370 1280 or 1-877 434 7268. Reservations can also be made on-line at www.discoverycove.com

Daily 9–5:30

Lunch in the Laguna Grill is included in the admission price; the Oasis snack cabanas (£) serve refreshments

I-Ride, Lynx #42

Swim with dolphins, rays and thousands of tropical fish then laze on the sand at this beach paradise created in landlocked Orlando.

To swim with dolphins is a cherished dream for millions of animal lovers worldwide, so it should come as no surprise that somebody in Orlando came up with the brilliant idea of creating a theme park where this particular dream can come true. Sister to the world-famous SeaWorld Orlando (▶ 21, 36–37) theme park across the road (and Busch Gardens in Tampa, ▶ 16, 48–50), Discovery Cove opened its doors in 2000 and has been so successful that the park has recently completed its first major expansion programme. Unlike other theme parks, which rely on a high turnover of guests, Discovery Cove aims for exclusivity. Admission is by advance reservation only and limited

Meeting a dolphin

Very good, includes wheelchairs adapted for sandy beaches

Very expensive; a reduced package is available for children 3–5 and guests who do not take part in the dolphin swim

The hands-on Trainer for a Day programme is available for up to 12 guests a day. Reservations essential

to 1,000 guests per day ensuring that the park is never over-run and the all-important dolphin-swim programme is not compromised. The all-inclusive tickets include a personal guide, unlimited access to all swim and snorkelling areas, the use of snorkel equipment, wetsuits, towels, lockers and beach chairs, plus a freshly prepared meal and a seven-day unlimited use pass to neighbouring SeaWorld Orlando.

The highlight of the day is undoubtedly the 45-minute dolphin swim (30 minutes of which are spent in the water though guests need not be strong swimmers), yet there is plenty more to see and do. Don a snorkel to explore a colourful manmade reef teeming with tropical fish and swim in the Ray Lagoon, then take time out on dry land to bask on the beach or visit the huge, free-flight aviary.

4
Fantasy of Flight

Vintage planes, each with a story to tell, help illustrate aviation history at this Central Florida aviation attraction.

The first thing to notice at Fantasy of Flight is the elegant 1930s and 1940s-style art deco themed buildings, designed to capture the spirit of aviation's Golden Era. Within the twin hangars and parked out on the runways are more than 20 vintage aircraft, just a part of the world's largest private collection built up over the last quarter century by aviation enthusiast Kermit Weeks.

The earliest authentic aircraft on display here, including a Sopwith Camel, date from World War I. However, illustrating the real dawn of flight, there is a reproduction of the Wright Brothers' 1903 Kitty Hawk Flyer, a cat's-cradle of wires and wooden struts, which has actually flown – if only for a few seconds at a time. A prime Golden Era exhibit with a notable history is the 1929 Ford Tri-Motor, launched by movie star Gloria Swanson. It flew across the US coast-to-coast in 48 hours and was later used in the making of *Indiana Jones and the Temple of Doom*.

The collection of World War II fighter planes from the US, Britain and Germany are among the museum's most popular exhibits, and visitors can test out their air combat skills in the Fightertown Flight Simulators, piloting their way through an aerial dogfight over the Pacific. Another themed 'immersion experience' is the History of Flight, which features walk-through dioramas. Backlot Tours take visitors behind the scenes to see the restoration workshops (weather permitting).

See also ► 53.

✚ 46A1

✉ SR559, Polk City (I-4 West to Exit 44)

☎ (863) 984 3500

🕐 Daily 9–5

🍴 Compass Rose (£–££)

♿ Good

✋ Expensive

❓ Call for details of hot air balloon and biplane rides

Fantasy of Flight, where the past comes to life

5
Kennedy Space Center

✚ 47D2

✉ SR405, Merritt Island (Bee Line Expressway/SR528 toll road east from Orlando)

☎ (321) 449 4444 or (321) 454 4198 TDD

🕐 Daily 9–dusk

🍴 Mila's (£–££); cafés and concessions (£)

♿ Very good

✋ Expensive

❓ Bus tours depart regularly (allow 2½ hours). Book for the IMAX cinemas at Spaceport Central on purchasing tickets

Tours, films, rockets and space hardware bring the American space programme to life at NASA's Florida space launch facility.

The Kennedy Space Center Visitor Complex is the gateway to Launch Complex 39, where today's space shuttles blast off into orbit, and where Apollo 11 set off on its ground-breaking journey to deliver the first man to walk on the moon in 1969. A visit to the Space Center offers a terrific opportunity to delve into the history of the US space programme, experience a nail-biting re-creation of the countdown to blast off, get a behind-the-scenes view of space technology and look at the shape of things to come.

The very first rockets launched from Cape Canaveral were long-range guided missiles fired from Cape Canaveral Air Force Station in the early 1950s. NASA, the National Aeronautics and Space Administration established in 1958 to carry out the peaceful exploration and use of space, later used the site to prepare and launch science satellites and the manned and unmanned flights of the early Mercury and Gemini programmes. In 1964, NASA transferred operations to Launch Complex 39, at Merritt Island, which was designed to handle the Apollo-Saturn V programme. The first launch from the Kennedy Space Center was the Apollo 8 mission in December 1968.

Today, bus tours offer views of the space shuttle launch pads, the gargantuan Vehicle Assembly Building (VAB) and make a stop at the spectacular $37-million Apollo/Saturn V Center. There is also access to the International Space Station (ISS) Center where the ISS is being constructed. Families with small children will probably find a half-day visit long enough.

See also ► 59.

The Space Shuttle exhibit comes highly recommended

6
SeaWorld Orlando

Shamu, the killer whale, star of SeaWorld, heads up an all-star cast at the world's most popular sea life park.

A walrus steals the show at SeaWorld

Laid out over an action-packed 200-acre site, SeaWorld provides a full day's itinerary of shows and marine encounters in the best theme park tradition. The stars of the shows are almost exclusively of the finned or flippered variety and their virtuoso performances (coaxed by the strategic deployment of a seemingly endless supply of fish) are a source of continuous amazement and delight to packed audiences. Though SeaWorld can get very busy, its built-in advantage over other traditional parks is the scarcity of rides, so there are few queues. This is good news, particularly for families with small children.

Shamu shows, performances in the Whale & Dolphin Stadium and the Sea Lion & Otter Stadium are a must. The Penguin Encounter (with real snow) should not be missed, and anybody who has never seen a manatee should rectify this immediately at Manatees: The Last Generation?.

Not surprisingly, SeaWorld pushes its role as a significant animal rescue, conservation and research facility. There are several entertaining and gently educational behind-the-scenes tours on offer for interested guests as well as summer camp adventures. For those looking for an even more interactive experience, SeaWorld's sister park, Discovery Cove, invites guests to swim with bottlenose dolphins and tropical fish (➤ 17, 32).

See also ➤ 36–7

✚ 46B2

✉ 7007 SeaWorld Drive, Orlando (I-4/Exit 71

☎ (407) 351 3600

🕐 Daily 9–7 (extended summer and hols).

🍴 Aloha Polynesian Luau, Dine With Shamu, Sharks Underwater Grill (£££), reservations ☎ 1-800 327 2424. Also assorted cafés, snack, BBQ and sandwich shops

🚌 I-Ride, Lynx #42

♿ Very good

✋ Very expensive. There is a 10 per cent discount for ticket purchases made over the internet (www.seaworld.com), or as part of the 4- and 5-Park Orlando Flex Tickets

7
Silver Springs

Boat trips, jeep safaris, animal encounters and popular music shows are all part of the deal at 'Florida's Original Attraction'.

All aboard the Silver Queen

 46A4

 SR40, 1 mile east of Ocala (72 miles northwest of Orlando)

☎ (352) 236 2121 or 1-800 234 7458

🕐 Daily 10–5 (extended summer and hols)

🍴 The Deli (£); Springside Pizzeria (£); Springside Restaurant (£–££); Swampy's Smokehouse Buffet (£–££); snack stops, ice creams and cold drinks stalls (£)

 Good

 Very expensive; no extra charge for concerts

 Ocala National Forest (► 62)

In 1878, Silver Springs entrepreneur Hullum Jones had a brainwave. He installed a glass viewing box in the flat bottom of a dugout canoe and invented the glass-bottomed boat tour, hence this popular nature park's claim to being the Sunshine State's first tourist attraction.

More than a century on, the glass-bottomed boat rides are as popular as ever, creating a window into an underwater world teeming with fish, turtles, crustaceans and ancient fossils at the head of the world's largest artesian spring formation. Visitors can also enjoy the Lost River Voyage, which plies the unspoilt Silver River, with a stop at a wildlife rescue outpost; or a Jungle Cruise on Fort King Waterway, where non-native animals look on.

Jeep safaris also do the jungle thing, four-wheeling through a 35-acre Florida jungle, where specially designed animal habitats include Big Gator Lagoon. Other top attractions include bear and panther exhibits.

Showtime at Silver Springs brings on the bugs and the creepy-crawlies at Creature Feature, an alarmingly up-close look at spiders and scorpions, toads and giant Madagascan hissing cockroaches. For something a little more wholesome, watch domestic cats and dogs performing tricks at the Amazing Pets displays. The park also attracts popular music acts for its annual weekend Concert Series starting in March.

See also ► 63.

8
Splendid China

*More than 60 of China's best-known scenic,
cultural and historic sites have been re-created in
meticulous miniature at this 76-acre site.*

Inspired by a similar park laid out in the southern Chinese city of Shenzen, Splendid China is a masterpiece in miniature. It took 120 Chinese artisans two years to complete the original project, using traditional craft methods dating back to the 14th century. The beautifully finished models of pagodas and palaces, and the half-mile-long one-tenth size version of the Great Wall, used up more than 6.5 million tiny bricks.

The craftsmen also built a scaled down army of Terracotta Warriors, based on the famous terracotta figures discovered guarding the tomb of the Qinshihuang emperor at Xi'an in 1974. The four-storey-high Leshan Grand Buddha Statue is a dainty replica of the 235-foot-high original which is carved into a mountain and can accommodate 10 men on each of its toes. Take a stroll around a fragment of the 65,765-acre petrified limestone Stone Forest found in Yunnan Province, and marvel at the elegant Summer Palace, where hundreds of colourful ceramic supplicants, soldiers and courtiers crowd the courtyards, and royal barges load up from marble jetties on the edge of a lagoon landscaped with twisted, lichen-spotted dwarf trees.

Splendid China is also famous for its shows featuring Chinese acrobats and dancers. The 90-minute spectaculars are a riot of exotic costumes and breathtaking agility and take place in the ornate Golden Peacock Theater.

See also ➤ 65.

✚ 29A1

✉ 3000 Spendid China Boulevard/NM 4.5, Kissimmee (3 miles west of I-4/Exit 25-B)

☎ (407) 396 7111 or 1-800 244 6226

🕐 Daily 9:30–7 (extended summer and hols)

🍴 Within park: The Great Wall Terrace (£–££); Wind and Rain Court (£–££); Pagoda Garden (£). Chinatown shopping area: Seven Flavours (£); Hong Kong Seafood Restaurant (£££)

♿ Very good

💷 Very expensive

↔ A World of Orchids (➤ 46)

❓ Guided walking tours and tours in motorised carts can be arranged for a fee

China's fabled Imperial Palace in the Forbidden City, re-created in miniature

9
Walt Disney World Resort

29A1

Walt Disney World Resort, Lake Buena Vista (I-4/Exits 25-B and 26-B, 20 miles south of Orlando)

(407) 824 4321

Check current schedules

Each park offers a wide choice of dining options open for breakfast, lunch, dinner, and snacks throughout the day. Priority seating ((407) 939 3463 or bookings service at Guest Relations) is advised for table service restaurants (££–£££)

Free shuttle bus services from many Orlando/Kissimmee hotels

Excellent

Very expensive

Details of daily parades, showtimes and nighttime fireworks and laser displays are printed in current park guides. Tickets are available on a one-day, one-park basis. For longer stay guests, a choice of multi-day passes offer greater flexibility and savings. They cover unlimited admission to any combination of theme parks, WDW Resort transportation, and limited admission to other Disney attractions such as the water parks, Pleasure Island, DisneyQuest and Disney's Wide World of Sports. Unused days never expire and can be used on a future visit.

This is the big one: Walt Disney's Florida showcase put Orlando on the map and has become a legend in its own short lifetime.

Walt Disney World Resort is the largest and most famous theme park resort in the world. Its 27,500-acre site is twice the size of Manhattan, and although only a small portion of this has been developed to date, it contains four major theme parks: Magic Kingdom, Epcot, Disney-MGM Studios, and Disney's Animal Kingdom, plus two water parks, a nightclub theme park within the huge lakefront Downtown Disney shopping, dining and entertainment district, themed resorts, gardens, lakes, championship golf courses and a professional sports complex.

Walt Disney opened his first theme park in Anaheim, California, in 1955. Disneyland, the prototype for the Magic Kingdom which now flourishes in Japan and France as well as Florida, was a huge success, but Disney was unable to control the explosion of hotels that popped up around the site and prevented him from expanding the park. Instead, he began to look for alternative locations and was drawn to Orlando for its climate, communications links and vast tracts of cheap farmland, which he began to purchase in secret during 1964. With 27,500 acres in the bag at a cost of around $5.5 million, Disney announced his plans to create 'a complete vacation environment' unsullied by low rent commercialism.

Disney died in 1966 without seeing his Florida vision completed. But The Walt Disney Company did him proud, producing Magic Kingdom in Disneyland's image. This opened in 1971, followed by Epcot (Experimental Prototype Community Of Tomorrow), a futuristic pet project devised by Disney which finally opened in 1985. Disney-MGM Studios was rushed out in 1989, months ahead of Universal Studios' mammoth Florida facility (➤ 26); and now Central Florida's animal-orientated parks are feeling the pinch as Disney's Animal Kingdom exercises its powerful Disney appeal on the public.

'Doing Disney' is quite an undertaking. There is so much to see that it is all too easy to overdo things, and first-time visitors are in danger of wearing themselves out with ambitious plans to see the lot in a couple of days. Take a tip from the repeat visitors who plan their itineraries with almost military precision, zero in on the best rides and avoid the restaurants at peak times. Never plan on doing more than one park a day, and if you are visiting all four theme parks during your stay, include at least one rest day. Cost is another important consideration: Disney does not come cheap. If money is no object, Walt Disney World Resort is without doubt the best place to stay, with a choice of fine hotels boasting excellent facilities and free transport to the parks. Package deals paid in advance to cover theme park tickets and accommodation in Walt Disney World Resort hotels are one way of avoiding a nasty shock. For budget travellers there is plenty of affordable accommodation near by in Kissimmee, or around Orlando's International Drive.

See also ➤ 70–90.

Cinderella Castle, Walt Disney World Resort's most famous landmark

Photograph: © Disney

10
Universal Orlando

✚ 29B2

✉ 1000 Universal Orlando Plaza, Orlando (I-4/Exit 74B or 75AB)

☎ (407) 363 8000 or 1-800 232 7827

🕐 Daily from 9AM; closing times vary

🍴 Both parks offer a choice of dining options, from snack stops and counter service cafés to full restaurants

♿ Very good

✋ Very expensive

↔ Wet 'n' Wild (➤ 43)

Filming a New York street scene

Blockbuster rides, shows and attractions recreate movie magic and comic strip heroes at Universal's two Florida theme parks.

Disney may have greater worldwide recognition, but for many visitors to Orlando – particularly adult and teenage thrillseekers – Universal delivers a more exciting theme park experience. The original, movie-orientated, Universal Studios Florida theme park opened in 1990, sharing a site with the largest working movie and television production facility outside Hollywood. It soon developed a worldwide reputation for innovative, state-of-the-art thrill rides, such as the groundbreaking 21-million giga-watt Back To The Future… The Ride simulator experience. More recently the excellent Terminator 2:3-D Battle Across Time, and the interactive MEN IN BLACK Alien Attack, have consolidated the park's global standing.

In 1999, Universal Studios Florida metamorphosed into Universal Orlando, a complete resort destination with on-site hotels, the 30-acre CityWalk shopping, dining and entertainment complex, and a second theme park, Islands of Adventure. Adrenaline junkies are in for a treat at Islands

of Adventure, which styles its roller-coaster and thrill rides after Marvel comic book heroes such as Spider-Man, Doctor Doom and the Incredible Hulk. A further range of entertaining rides and shows features the likes of Sinbad the Sailor, Jurassic Park's dinosaurs, children's favourites Dr Seuss and Popeye.

After dark, all the action moves to CityWalk, which boasts the world's biggest Hard Rock Café, attached to a 2,200-seat auditorium, a movie megaplex, shopping, nightclubs, jazz, and a wide variety of themed restaurants, ranging from a NASCAR Café for motorsports fans to a very laidback Key West-styled Jimmy Buffett's Margaritaville.

See also ➤ 38–43.

What To See

Above: *gourmet food*
Right: *Busch Gardens*

27

Orlando

In the 1930s, traffic signals in downtown Orlando wore a sign admonishing drivers to be quiet. There were fresh fruit juice stands on the sidewalk and the city resembled 'a great, cultivated park'. Since Orlando has become synonymous with theme parks, it is generally assumed to be a loud, brash place.

Living in the shadow of the Mouse has certainly brought radical changes. The mini-Manhattan of the downtown district is bounded by highways, and the sky is busy with jets coming to and going from the international airport. But the city of Orlando has not succumbed entirely to the trappings of the tourist industry. There are pockets of greenery in Lake Eola and Harry P. Leu Gardens, and recent developments have included the renovated historic district around downtonw Church Street, the Orlando Science Center and its satellite art and history museums, and the palatial Orange County Convention Center.

> *'Orlando has been a favorite resort for a type of visitor ... [who] believes his health and longevity depend upon orange juice and the local brand of sunshine.'*
>
> The WPA Guide to Florida
> (1939)

Orlando

Orlando's untidy outline sprawls either side of I-4, the fast interstate highway which slices across Central Florida from the Gulf of Mexico to the Atlantic Coast.

The city has extended steadily southwest towards Walt Disney World Resort and Kissimmee, and most visitors who stay in Orlando are based south of the city in the International Drive resort area. SeaWorld, Discovery Cove and Universal Orlando are just off I-Drive (as International Drive is familiarly called), which is served by the I-Ride bus.

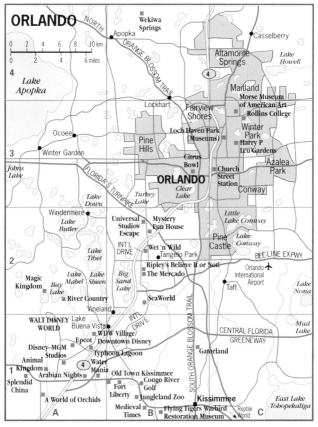

29

Opposite: *white sand beaches and tropical lagoons at Discovery Cove*

What to See in Orlando

It may come as a suprise to the vast majority of visitors who never venture beyond the distinctly touristy environs of I-Drive and the major theme parks, but Orlando does have more to offer than the well-travelled strip of hotels, motels, discount malls and smaller attractions that constitute the city's main resort area. This section deals with Orlando itself, while charming Winter Park, neighbouring Kissimmee, and other attractions further afield are covered in Around Orlando ➤ 45–69.

DISCOVERY COVE ✪✪✪

✚ 29B2
✉ 6000 Discovery Cove Way (I-4/Exit 71 or 72)
☎ (407) 370 1280 or 1-877 434 7268. reservations can also be made on-line at www.discoverycove.com
🕑 Daily 9–5:30
🍴 Lunch in the Laguna Grill included; snack cabanas (£)
♿ Very good, includes wheelchairs adapted for sandy beaches
💷 Very expensive, minimum age for dolphin swim is 6; a reduced price package is available for cildren 3–5 and guests who do not take part in the dolphin swim
❓ Advanced reservations essential for the Trainer Day programme

A limited admission, by reservation-only, marine park adjacent to its big sister attraction SeaWorld (➤ 21, 36–7), Discovery Cove offers a whole day's worth of marine encounters as well as its dolphin-swim experience. Created on a far more intimate scale than the traditional Orlando mega-parks, Discovery Cove prides itself on the personal touch with impressive service levels including one member of staff to every eight guests.

The kid gloves treatment begins at the check-in where guests are greeted by their personal guide and taken on an orientation tour. For the dolphin-swim in one of the three large lagoons, small groups of six to eight guests (three to four groups per lagoon) and a trainer wade into shallow water to meet the dolphins and learn some of the hand signals the trainers use to communicate with their 30 or so Atlantic bottlenose charges. The group then moves into a deep-water lagoon for one-to-one swimming and playing with the friendly mamals.

The marine thrills aren't over yet. Guests can snorkel amongst thousands of tropical reef fish from 90 different species in a coral reef setting, while sharks and barracudas patrol just a few inches away behind plexiglass safety panels. At Ray Lagoon wade into a world of sleek and mysterious rays as dozens of southern and cownose stingrays, which can grow up to 4ft across, glide past to be touched and fed little snacks. There is plenty of space to

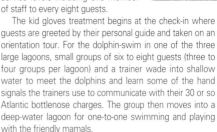

relax on the newly extended sandy beaches around the resort-style swimming pool. Some 5,000 tons of sand have been imported to lend that all important realistic feel to the scene with its beach chairs and colourful cabanas. Another option is to take a gentle meander down Tropical River. The river flows at a lazy 5–7mph past sunken ruins and hidden grottoes, waterfalls and beaches to the 12,000 square foot aviary. This lushly landscaped free-flight enclosure, with its waterfall centrepiece, houses around 300 birds from the tiny finches and hummingbirds to substantial toucans and elegant demoiselle cranes.

For guests anxious to get behind the scenes, the park offers a Trainer for a Day programme for just 12 guests a day at an additional fee. Participants get to work side-by-side with Discovery Cove animal experts as they work with dolphins, sharks, stingrays and birds as well as mammals such as sloths and anteaters from the nature walk at the entrance to the park.

GATORLAND ⬤⬤

Southeast of Orlando, on the border with Kissimmee, a pair of giant alligator jaws forms the entrance to this classic Florida attraction. Hundreds of captive 'gators' occupy various pens and pools. There are alligator shows, alligator meals (try Gator Nuggets in Pearl's Smokehouse), and alligator products, such as wallets, boots and handbags, on sale in the gift shop. Other Gatorland residents include Florida crocodiles and caymans, native snapping and soft-shell turtles, and snake displays feature venomous rattlesnakes and cottontail moccasins.

A highlight of the park is the 2,000-foot-long marshland boardwalk edging a cypress swamp. This is a native habitat alligator breeding ground and a fabulous birdwatching spot. In spring, snowy egrets construct their twiggy nests within a few feet of passers-by, and there are great and little blue herons, pigeon-sized little green herons and dozens of other wading birds living in the water's edge rookeries.

HARRY P. LEU GARDENS ⬤⬤⬤

Sloping gently down to the shores of Lake Rowena, these lovely 50-acre gardens provide a soothing escape from the hustle and bustle. They were originally laid out by local businessman Harry P. Leu and his wife, who purchased the property in 1936 and lived in historic Leu House, a much-enlarged pioneer home in the middle of the gardens.

Near the entrance, the lush Ravine Garden leads down to a boardwalk and a gazebo which overlooks the lake. Coots and ducks potter about in the lake's waters and the occasional wild alligator lurks here. To the west of the property, mature southern magnolias and spreading live oaks shade the camellia woods, which can be seen at their

best during the October to March flowering season. The Leus planted more than 2,000 camellia specimens here, and their collection is considered to be one of the finest in the eastern US.

The floral centrepiece is the Rose Garden, a popular setting for open-air weddings among the 1,000 scented rose bushes. Close by, Leu House is open for regular tours. In the far corner of the gardens, the Display Greenhouse is a riot of hothouse orchids, tropical gingers, anthuriums, heliconias and ferns.

Above: *one of Gatorland's scaly residents*
Left: *a giant pair of alligator jaws from the entrance to gatorland*

HERITAGE SQUARE

A focus for downtown Orlando, the Heritage Square development has been designed to symbolise 'the heart of the community'. This is the site where the city's early pioneers would have plotted out the land and planned its development. The old Orange County Courthouse is here, recently refurbished to house the Orange County Regional History Centre (➤ 34), and the almost 2-acre park and plaza has been attractively landscaped with native trees, plants and Floridian-inspired landmarks as well as a pop-jet fountain which is a magnet for children.

✚ 29C3
✉ Central Boulevard at Magnolia Avenue (I-4 to exit 82C/Anderson Street)
↔ Orange County Regional History Center (➤ 34)

MENNELLO MUSEUM

Florida's only folk art museum and a delightful find for fans of the genre. The workds of Earl Cunningham (1893–1977) form the basis of the collections courtesy of lorida collectors Michael and Marilyn Mennello, who are donating 44 of Cunningham's works to the museum over 13 years. Cunningham, who could list chicken farmer, seaman and junk dealer amongst his former careers, favoured 'historical-fantasy' themes and his colourful palette adapts superbly to exuberant depictions of typically Floridian scenes from florious Technicolour sunsets and native birdlife to Seminole villages and lively marine paintings featuring his favourite early 20th-century schooners. The museum also hosts regular visiting exhibitions of modern and antique paintings and sculpture.

✚
✉ 900 E Princeton Street (I-4 to exit 85)
☎ (407) 246 4278
🕐 Tue–Sat 11–5, Sun 12–5. Closed Mon
♿ Good
💲 Cheap
↔ Harry P. Leu Gardens (above), Orlando Museum of Art (➤ 34), Orlando Science Center (➤ 35)

ORANGE COUNTY REGIONAL HISTORY CENTER ⭐⭐

Step back 12,000 years in the heart of downtown Orlando and let the Regional History Center put the case for life in Central Florida pre-Mouse. Set in the handsomely restored 1927 Orange County Courthouse on Heritage Square (➤ 32), the Center recalls Central Florida history through imaginatively designed audio and visual presentations as well as hands-on exhibits. Visitors are greeted by The Dome, a three-dimensional showcase for Florida icons, followed by an orientation experience. Suitably immersed in local lore, exhibits whisk you back in time to the Paleo-Indian era and a Timucuan village, the arrival of the Spanish explorers, a pioneer Cracker homestead, and the Roaring 20s when Tin Can tourists in Model-T Fords descended on Florida in their thousands. Natural history, the citrus industry, Disney and NASA all get a look in too.

🔲 29C3
✉ One Heritage Square, 65 E Central Boulevard (I-4 to Exit 82C/Anderson Street)
☎ (407) 836 8500
🕐 Mon–Sat 10–5, Sun 12–5
♿ Good
💵 Moderate
↔ Heritage Square (➤ 32)

Right: *Orlando Museum of Art has a renowned pre-Columbian collection* Opposite: *Vincent van Gogh's Self-Portrait in Front of an Easel created from 10,000 picture postcards at Ripley's Believe It or Not!*

🔲 29C3
✉ Loch Haven Park, E Princeton Street (I-4/Exit 85)
☎ (407) 896 4231
🕐 Tue–Sat 10–5, Sun 12–5. Closed Mon
♿ Good
💵 Cheap
↔ Harry P. Leu Gardens (➤ 33), Orlando Science Center (➤ 35)

ORLANDO MUSEUM OF ART ⭐

The museum invites tourists to experience Orlando's cultural side and frequently hosts touring art shows, so check current schedules. If the permanent collections are on show, visitors will be rewarded with a notable collection of pre-Columbian art – some 250 pieces dating from around 1200 BC to AD 1500 – plus works by leading 19th- to 20th-century American artists and African art exhibits.

ORLANDO SCIENCE CENTER ⊕⊕

Topped by a distinctive silver observatory dome, Orlando's impressive Science Center opened its doors in 1997. The exhibits are laid out over four levels and include dozens of interactive displays and hands-on educational games designed to appeal to children of all ages – and not a few adults as well.

On ground level, the NatureWorks Florida habitat section combines models and living exhibits such as turtles, baby alligators and a reef tank, and there is the excellent KidsTown early learning area for 8s and under. On Levels 2, 3 and 4, more elaborate and sophisticated exhibits tackle the basics of physics, mathematics, applied technologies and human biology in comprehensible and entertaining style. Movie moguls should definitely see the TechWorks exhibit on Level 4, which explores the behind-the-scenes tricks of the movie trade.

In addition, there are daily science-orientated shows in the Darden Adventure Theater and the Digistar Planetarium, and large format film presentations in the CineDome, which boasts a massive 8,000 square-foot IMAX screen. On Friday and Saturday nights, while the CineDome features 3-D laser light shows, the Observatory welcomes star-gazers.

RIPLEY'S BELIEVE IT ⊕ OR NOT! ORLANDO ODDITORIUM

A whacky, lop-sided building tipping down an imaginary sinkhole, a hologram greeting from the long-dead Robert L Ripley and hundreds of curious, eccentric and downright bizarre exhibits add up to a fairly unbelievable attraction. Robert Ripley was a connoisseur of oddities. Travelling extensively in the 1920s and 1930s, he amassed enough material to stock more than a dozen 'museums' of this type worldwide. Typical exhibits include a Mona Lisa made from 1,426 squares of toast and a three-quarter scale model of a 1907 Rolls Royce Silver Ghost made out of 1,016,711 matchsticks and 63 pints of glue.

🚩 29C3
✉ 777 E Princeton Street (I-4/Exit 85)
☎ (407) 514 2000
🕐 Tue–Thu 9–5, Fri–Sat 9–9, Sun 12–5. Closed Mon, Thanksgiving and Christmas
🍴 OSC Cafe (£)
♿ Very good
💰 Moderate
↔ Harry P. Leu Gardens (► 33), Orlando Museum of Art (► 34)

🚩 29B2
✉ 8201 International Drive
☎ (407) 345 0501 or 1-800 998 4418
🕐 Daily 9AM–1AM
♿ Good
🚌 I-Ride, Lynx #42
💰 Moderate

✚ 29B2

✉ 7007 SeaWorld Drive, Orlando (I-4/Exit 71 or72)

☎ (407) 351 3600

🕐 Daily 9–7 (extended summer and hols)

🍽 Nine restaurants ranging from cafeteria-style to full service (£–£££), plus snack stops. Reservations for Dine With Shamu, Sharks Underwater Grill and Aloha Polynesian Luau Dinner and Show should be made in advance on ☎ 1-800 327 2424

🚌 I-Ride, Lynx #42

♿ Very good

🎟 Orlando FlexTickets offer reduced rates and flexibility. Available from participating parks, 4-Park tickets provide unlimited admission to SeaWorld Orlando, Universal Orlando and Wet 'n' Wild. 5-Park tickets include Busch Gardens in Tampa

❓ Guided tours of Terrors of the Deep, Wild Arctic and the animal rescue and research facility can be made at the Guided Tours counter near the entrance. For Sharks Deep Dive, the False Killer Whale, Animal Care and Trainer for a Day programmes, plus the guided Adventure Express Tour of the park, advance reservations are recommended, ☎ 1-800 432 1178 (press 5)

SEAWORLD ORLANDO ✪✪✪

SeaWorld's well-balanced combination of sights and shows is a proven winner. Unlike some parks, where the shows are incidental to the main action, here they are an intrinsic ingredient, and the rest of the attractions – plus behind-the-scenes tours (➤ panel) – can be fitted in as visitors make their way around the many and various show stadiums.

Unusual dining options in the park include Dine with Shamu and Sharks Underwater Grill. Sunset reveals another side of SeaWorld, with nightly laser and fireworks displays and the **Aloha Polynesian Luau Dinner and Show** .

Below is a list of highlights; see also ➤ 21.

Cydesdale Hamlet Theme park owners and brewers Anheuser-Busch maintain a pristine stable area for their giant Scottish Clydesdale draft horses. The Anheuser-Busch Hospitality Center is here, too.

Journey to Atlantis Rickety Greek fishing boats transport guests on a sight-seeing trip to the newly risen City of Atlantis when disaster strikes and a high-speed water ride with special effects ensues.

Key West at Sea World A Florida Keys themed area, with a tropical atmosphere and street performers. The centrepiece is two-acre Dolphin Cove, a lagoon habitat for Atlantic bottlenose dolphins adjacent to the Whale & Dolphin Stadium. Rescued turtles bask on the rocks of Turtle Point, visitors can feed and pet captive stingrays in the Stingray Lagoon, and there are nightly festivities in Sunset Square.

Kraken More thrills aboard a mega sea serpent-styled roller-coaster.

Manatees: The Last Generation? A distant aquatic relative of the elephant, the manatee is now a seriously endangered species. There may be fewer than 2,000 of these giant Florida sea cows left in the wild.

All the manatees in this SeaWorld exhibit are rescued and will be returned to the wild if possible.

Pacific Point Preserve California sea lions, harbour seals and South American fur seals occupy this rocky northern Pacific coast re-creation, complete with wave machine.

Penguin Encounter Some 200 enchanting Antarctic penguins and their Arctic cousins, the alcids (better known as puffins and mures), inhabit these icy confines.

Shamu Adventure An introduction to the world of the killer whale hosted by animal expert Jack Hanna. Makes a good preface to the Shamu stadium shows.

Shamu's Happy Harbor Play area for small children with climbing apparatus, radio-controlled boats, a sandpit and face-painting activities.

Terrors of the Deep Scene-setting, spooky music and eerie lighting accompany these aquariums full of lurking moray eels, 28mph barracudas and highly toxic puffer fish. Ride the perspex tunnel through the 660,000-gallon shark tank, or get really up close and personal with the park's daring interaction programme, Sharks Deep Dive, and don a wesuit for a ride through the habitat in a shark cage.

Wild Arctic A simulated helicopter ride transports visitors to an Arctic base station for close encounters with polar bears, beluga whales and walruses. However, the icy habitats appear distinctly cramped for these large animals.

Below: a *fascinating underwater exhibit provides a clear view of all the drama and action of the sea*
Inset: *killer whales on form at SeaWorld*

*The famous Universal
Studios globe symbol
appears to rotate in a
fountain at the main
entrance*

 29B2

✉ 1000 Universal Plaza,
Orlando (I-4/Exit 74B or
75AB)

☎ (407) 224 6735 or 10877
837 2273

🕐 Daily from 9AM; closing
times vary

🍴 Both parks offer a choice
of dining options from
snack stops and counter
service cafés to full
service restaurants

♿ Very good

💰 Very expensive.
Orlando FlexTickets offer
reduced rates and
flexibility. Available from
participating parks,
4-Park tickets provide
unlimited admission to
SeaWorld Orlando,
Universal Studios Escape
and Wet 'n Wild over 14
consecutive days. 5-Park
tickets include Busch
Gardens in Tampa. For
further information ☎ 1-
800 224 3838.

↔ Wet 'n' Wild (➤ 43)

UNIVERSAL ORLANDO ✪✪✪
Ride though the movies at Universal Studios and escape to
the fantasy world of legends and comic book heroes at
Islands of Adventure. These two top theme parks are the
twin poles of the Universal Orlando resort.

See also ➤ 26.

UNIVERSAL STUDIOS
It would be a mistake to assume that if you have done
Walt Disney World Resort's Disney-MGM Studios
(➤ 77–9) you should skip this. The Universal experience is
more ride-orientated than its Disney rival and the attractive
layout is a definite plus.

The most popular shows on the Universal lot include
the Wild, Wild, Wild West Stunt Show; Beetlejuice's
Graveyard Revue; Blues Brothers soul-style entertainment;
and Animal Planet Live!, a spin-off of a popular US TV
show showcasing talented animals.

Below is a list of highlights.

Alfred Hitchcock: The Art of Making Movies An educa-
tional behind-the-scenes homage to the master of
Hollywood suspense, with screen presentations by
Hitchcock himself.
Back to the Future…The Ride One of the most ambitious
theme park rides ever created, this four-minute, spin in
Doc Brown's time-travelling DeLorean is a must, with its
wild simulator action and 70mm IMAX screens.
Earthquake: The Big One It is a short step off the San
Francisco street set to this subway journey from hell.
Experience an 8.3 on the Richter Scale, as portrayed in the
classic 1974 disaster movie *Earthquake*.
ET Adventure A gentle ride over 3,340 miniature buildings
aboard flying bicycles with ET in a basket on the front
handlebars. A ride that appeals to younger children. .
Jaws Set amidst the seaside architecture and artfully
arranged lobster pots of a re-created fishing village,
Captain Jake's Amity Boat Tours embark for a wholly
expected watery encounter with the glistening jaws of
Universal's famous 32-foot, three-ton mechanical great

white shark. The steel-and-fibreglass shark moves at speeds of up to 20 feet per second, with a thrust power equal to a 727 jet engine. Passengers still love it, and this is a particularly attractive corner of the park.

Jimmy Neutron: Boy Genius A nickelodeon children's TV animated favourite, Jimmy has lept from small to large screen and now merits his very own theme park ride. Bucket alon in the boy genius' Rocket Pod to rescue the world from evil egg-shaped Yokian aliens.

Below: *face-to-face with Jaws*
Bottom: *the world's first life-size, ride-through video game – MEN IN BLACK Alien Attack*

MEN IN BLACK Alien Attack An interactive chase through the streets of New York in hot pursuit of invading aliens. Terrific techno-futuristic styling, wild manoeuvres and weapons that rack up your score from hero to loser.

Nickelodeon Studios World Headquarters
The nerve centre for America's top kid-tested and kid-approved children's television network. The soundstage tour is a bit long-winded, though the visit to the Gak Kitchen, where sublimely oozy, gloppy dollops of top-quality slime and goo are tested on willing young human guinea pigs, is a favourite stop. Then it's on to the Game Lab for some audience participation, testing new games.

Shrek An all-new adventure for the swamp-dwelling ogre and his lovely bride, Princess Fiona. Share the couple's honeymoon on 4-D 'Ogrevision' complete with multi-sensory effects (including alarming pneumatic seats). Inaugurated in spring

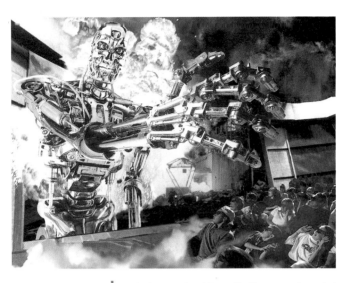

Above: *no expense was spared creating the 3-D effects for T2:3-D*

2003, the attraction picks up Shrek's story at the end of the first Shrek film and acts as a bridge to the upcoming sequel.

Terminator 2: 3-D Battle Across Time The world's first 3-D virtual adventure, 'T2:3-D' (to aficionados) reunited the *Terminator 2* team to produce the most expensive film, frame for frame, ever made: $24 million for 12 minutes. The audience is transported into an apocalyptic world, showered with 3-D flying debris and whirlygig mini-hunter pocket gunships, and menaced by the flexi-steel pincers of the re-generating T-1,000,000. Fantastic effects: not to be missed, however long the queue.

Twister… Ride It Out Lifted from the blockbuster movie, this multi-million dollar tornado encounter is not for the faint-hearted. Brave a five-storey-high cyclone, complete with torrential rain and howling winds.

Woody Woodpecker's KidZone A child-friendly zone of scaled down rides, adventure play areas and shows to delight the very young. Teeny thrills on Woody Woodpecker's Nuthouse Coaster, sing-a-long with the dinky dinosaurs in A Day In The Park With Barney, let off steam in Fievel's Playland or cool down amongst the water jets of the inter-active Curious George Goes to Town play area.

Above: *fun for youngsters on Woody Woodpecker's Nuthouse Coaster*

ISLANDS OF ADVENTURE

Universal employed the creative genius of movie director Steven Spielberg to help bring favourite comic strip characters and mythical legends to life in their second Florida theme park. Islands of Adventure claims to be the most technologically advanced theme park in the world combining a host of hair-raising rides and boldly drawn, imaginative surroundings. Unlike its sister park, where the rides and attractions bear little relation to the stylised districts they inhabit, Islands of Adventure has five distinctively themed 'islands' linked by footbridges and water transport from the Port of Entry. The park's highlights are listed island by island below.

Jurassic Park A lushly landscaped 'island' with a familiar theme based on Spielberg's blockbuster movie. Enjoy an overview of the district from the Pteranodon Flyers aerial runway; get up close and personal with an extraordinarily lifelike 'animatronic' dinosaur at the Triceratops Encounter; and prepare to ride the Jurassic Park River Adventure past a further collection of cunningly constructed prehistoric creatures with a dramatic 85-foot waterfall plunge as a finale.

Lost Continent A mythical world lost in the mists of time, the Lost Continent draws its inspiration from tales of Greek gods, Arthurian legend and the Arabian Nights. Dominating the skyline is Dueling Dragons, an intricately designed twin roller-coaster featuring a convincing near-miss scenario; young children are relegated to the scaled-down Flying Unicorn coaster nearby. There are action-packed thrills, stunts and towering pyrotechnic effects involved in The Eighth Voyage of Sindbad show, but the most elaborate attraction here is Poseidon's Fury: Escape From The Lost City entered via a swirling water vortex hurling 17,500 gallons of water around a 42-foot tunnel. The subsequent battle between the water god and his archrival, Zeus, employs a further 35,000 gallons of water and 200 flame effects.

Marvel Super Hero Island Universal's 21st-century technology has been used to create three state-of-the-art thrill rides in this primary-coloured, larger-than-life land fit for super heroes.

Above: watch a Raptor hatch at the Jurassic Park Discovery Center

Below: the Incredible Hulk Coaster at Marvel Super Hero Island

Overhead, the giant green Incredible Hulk Coaster (it glows in the dark) blasts riders from 0 to 40 mph in two seconds – equivalent to the G-force experienced by the pilot of an F-16 fighter jet – before embarking on a heartline inversion, seven roll-overs and two subterranean plunges. Across the street, guests are shot to the top of the twin 200-foot steel towers of Doctor Doom's Fearfall before plummeting back down to earth. There is plenty of techno wizardry on display at The Amazing Adventures of Spider-Man, which combines moving ride vehicles, spooky 3-D action and special effects in a running battle with the forces of evil out to kidnap the Statue of Liberty; and there is more special effects action in the Storm Force show spectacular.

Seuss Landing From optimum thrills to the whimsical world of Dr. Seuss, this

island is especially geared towards smaller children. An assortment of suitably bizarre Seussian creatures serve as mounts on the Caro-Seuss-el, reputed to be the most elaborate carousel ever built. The One Fish Two Fish Red Fish Blue Fish ride invites guests to steer their own guppy through a series of water features guided by a special rhyme: lose the rhyme and get doused by a squirt post. If I Ran The Zoo is an interactive play area; while the best ride for accompanying adults is The Cat In The Hat, an entertaining journey through scenes from the classic story enlivened by special effects.

Toon Lagoon Betty Boop, Beetle Bailey and Hagar the Horrible leap out of two-dimensions and into outsize 'life' on Comic Strip Lane, the main drag of Toon Lagoon. The lagoon in question is home to Me Ship, The Olive, a child-friendly play area aboard Popeye the Sailor's galleon. A short stroll away, Popeye & Bluto's Bilge-Rat Barges shoot the rapids in a whitewater raft ride that offers an ideal way to cool down on a hot day. And for a distinctly splashy flume ride, the first ever to send passengers below water level, sit tight for Dudley Do-Right's Ripsaw Falls.

Top left: The Cat in the Hat welcomes visitors to the If I Ran the Zoo play area

Bottom left: Wet 'n Wild claims more rides than any other water park in Florida

WET 'N WILD

The hottest way to cool off on International Drive, this 25-acre landmark water park offers dozens of thrills and spills, a scaled-down Kid's Park pool area and sunbathing decks. Top-rated heart-stopper is The Storm, a swirling body coaster with high speed chutes that lead into a wild whirl around a bowl and a splash landing. Other favourites include the 500-foot twisting descent of the Black Hole, in total darkness; the seven-storey Bomb Bay drop, and Der Stuka, one of the highest, fastest waterslides in the world. Meanwhile, family-sized inflatables tackle The Surge and Bubba Tub, or you can drift down Lazy River on a giant inner tube.

➕ 29B2
✉ 6200 International Drive (I-4/Exit 75AB)
☎ (407) 351 1800 or 1-800 992 9453
🕐 Daily, variable hours from 9AM in summer (10AM winter); call for schedules
🍴 Concessions (£)
🚌 I-Ride, Lynx #42
♿ Few
💲 Expensive.
Orlando FlexTickets offer reduced rates and flexibility. Available from participating parks, 4-Park tickets provide unlimited admission to SeaWorld Orlando, Universal Orlando (2) and Wet 'n Wild over 14 consecutive days. 5-Park tickets include Busch Gardens in Tampa
↔ Universal Orlando (➤ 26, 38–43)

Quality Inn

GREAT SERVICE

KEY W. KOLS

SEAFOOD · STEAK

BREAKFAST

99

Around Orlando

An all-but-invisible line divides Greater Orlando from neighbouring Kissimmee. Walt Disney World has transformed the former cattle town, bringing a welter of budget hotels and low-priced attractions along US192. Kissimmee is no beauty, but it is a useful family resort area, where the prices are fair, there are over 40,000 accommodation options and the entertainment is on tap.

Beyond Orlando and Kissimmee, Central Florida offers a wide choice of attractive day trips. Fast highways lead to top sightseeing destinations such as the Kennedy Space Center on the Atlantic coast and Tampa's Busch Gardens. Equally accessible are the horticultural highlights of Cypress Gardens and Bok Tower Gardens, and there are unspoilt state park preserves where hiking trails, canoe runs and wildlife-spotting provide the perfect antidote to the hurly-burly of the theme parks.

> *'Central Florida – a study in reality suspension, brought to your imagination by the nation's finest fantasy makers.'*
>
> FLORIDA TOURIST BOARD

———————●———————

Left: *larger-than-life signs line the street in Kissimmee*

Colourful blooms at
A World of Orchids

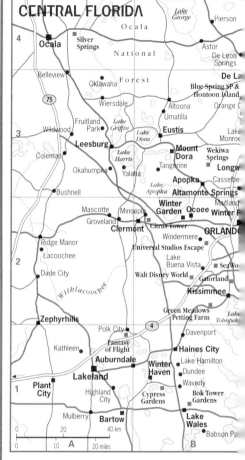

What to See Around Orlando

A WORLD OF ORCHIDS

Harboured in a half-acre, climate-controlled greenhouse jungle, the world's largest permanent indoor display of flowering orchids is quite a sight. There are more than 2,000 orchid species on view and they come in an incredible array of colours, shapes, sizes and delicate scents, set against a lush backdrop of exuberant tropical foliage, gingers, palms and dramatic bird-of-paradise flowers. It is worth taking one of the daily guided tours (11 and 3; also 1 on weekends). Outside, native Floridian orchids can be seen from the short boardwalk nature trail; there is a catfish angling pool and exotic bird displays.

29A1

2501 Old Lake Wilson
Road/CR545 (GM 5.5),
Kissimmee

(407) 396 1887

Tue–Sun 9:30–4:30.
Closed New Year's Day, 4
July, 2nd and 3rd weeks
in July, Thanksgiving,
Christmas Day

Few   Free

Splendid China (➤ 23, 65)

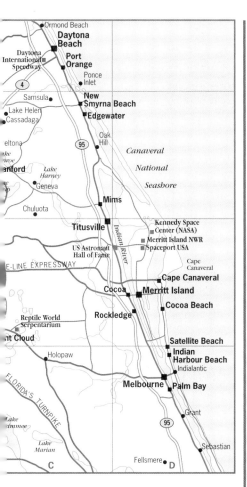

Ormond Beach
Daytona Beach
Daytona International Speedway
Port Orange
Ponce Inlet
Samsula
Lake Helen
Cassadaga
4
eltona
ke
rve
anford
Lake Harney
Geneva
New Smyrna Beach
Edgewater
Oak Hill
95
Canaveral National Seashore
Chuluota
Mims
Titusville
Kennedy Space Center (NASA)
Merritt Island NWR
Spaceport USA
US Astronaut Hall of Fame
Indian River
Cape Canaveral
E-LINE EXPRESSWAY
Cape Canaveral
Cocoa **Merritt Island**
Cocoa Beach
Reptile World Serpentarium
Rockledge
nt Cloud
Holopaw
Satellite Beach
Indian Harbour Beach
Indialantic
FLORIDA'S TURNPIKE
Melbourne **Palm Bay**
Lake immee
Grant
Lake Marian
95
C
Sebastian
Fellsmere D

Elegant Bok Tower, on the Florida peninsula's highest point, Iron Mountain

BOK TOWER GARDENS ✪✪✪

A short drive from the more overt charms of Cypress Gardens, these lovely woodland gardens are a real haven of peace and quiet. Dutch philanthropist Edward W Bok created the gardens in the 1920s and added the coquina rock and marble bell tower, with its world-class carillon. The tower is perched on top of Iron Mountain, the highest point on the Florida peninsula, at a modest 298 feet above sea level, and the gently sloping 157-acre gardens contain thousands of flowering azaleas, camellias and magnolias beneath a canopy of oaks, palms and pines. There are daily carillon recitals and tours of the elegant 1930s Mediterranean Revival-style Pinewood House and Gardens in the grounds on certain days.

➕ 46B1
✉ CR17-A (off Alt. 27, 3 miles north of Lake Wales)
☎ (863) 676 1408
🕐 Daily 8–5
🍴 Garden Restaurant (£)
♿ Good
✋ Moderate
↔ Cypress Gardens (► 18, 52), Lake Wales (► 61)
❓ Daily carillon recitals at 3PM; concerts for special events.

47

🕂 46A1

✉ Busch Boulevard, Tampa
(75 miles west of Orlando
via I-4 West and I-75
North to Fowler
Avenue/Exit 54)

☎ (813) 987 5082 or 1-888
800 5447

🕐 Daily 10–6 (extended
summer and hols)

🍴 Refreshment stops
throughout park, plus:
Zagora Café (Morocco);
Das Festhaus (Timbuktu);
Crown Colony Restaurant
(Crown Colony); Vivi
Storehouse Restaurant
(Congo); Stanleyville
Smokehouse
(Stanleyville); Hospitality
House (Bird Gardens)
(£–££)

♿ Very good

💰 Very expensive.
Orlando FlexTickets offer
reduced rates and
flexibility. Available from
participating parks, 4-Park
tickets provide unlimited
admission to SeaWorld
Orlando, Universal
Orlando (2) and Wet 'n
Wild over 14 consecutive
days. 5-Park tickets
include Busch Gardens in
Tampa. The park also
offers a range of behind-
the-scenes tours for an
additional charge. A guide
leads groups of up to 15
people on 4–5hr Guided
Adventure Tours; 30-
minute Serengeti safaris
allow closer contact with
the animals; and groups
of 7–10 participate in
feeding and training
encounters on Animal
Adventure tours.
Advance reservations:
www.buschgardens.com

❓ Check daily schedules for
show times

BUSCH GARDENS ✪✪✪

A popular side trip from Orlando, Busch Gardens provides a full day's family entertainment in a sprawling, African-inspired zoo-cum-theme park complex. The 10 themed areas each offer a choice of attractions. The excellent water rides are very wet, and rainproof capes are on sale, but few sunbaked visitors bother. However, it is a good idea to bring a change of clothes to avoid an uncomfortably soggy journey back to Orlando.

Opposite the Busch Gardens complex, Anheuser-Busch also operate a popular 36-acre water park, Adventure Island (summer only).

Below is a list of highlights; see also ➤ 16.

Bird Gardens Flamingos, ducks, ibis and koi fish do battle with screeching gulls for titbits in the leafy lagoon areas of the Bird Gardens. There is a walk-through aviary, an eagle exhibit, bird shows, and captive koala bears. On the edge of Bird Gardens, the duelling Gwazi roller-coaster rumbles over its 7,000 feet of wooden track.

Congo An action-packed area at the northern extent of the park, the Congo's attractions include the hair-raising Kumba roller coaster. The slightly less dramatic Python still manages two 360° loops and a 70-foot plunge. A drenching is guaranteed on the Congo River Rapids, and onlookers can man the Waterblasters on the bridge (25c a shot). The Ubanga-Banga Bumper Cars are located here, too; the Serengeti Express Railroad train stops at the station; and the park's magnificent Bengal tigers are incarcerated on undersized Claw Island.

Crown Colony Here you can eat at the park's only full-service dining room, the Crown Colony Restaurant; look in on the Anheuser-Busch brewery's ceremonial draft horses, and take a ride on Akbar Adventure Tours; a stomach-churning simulator ride.

Egypt Ruined columns, giant carved figures and hiero-glyphics provide the setting for a journey into Tut's Tomb, a walk-through tour of a replica pyramid tomb as discovered by the archaeologist Howard Carter in the 1920s. The contemporary news reel footage is fun, but the jewels look a little pasty. The big ride here is the 3,983-foot-long, 150-foot-high Montu roller coaster, featuring a heart-stopping inverted loop of 104ft. The Serengeti Express Railroad train travels across the Serengeti Plain.

Land of the Dragons A well-designed adventure playground for small children, with a friendly dragon theme. The three-storey Dragon's Nest treehouse is lavishly equipped with stairs and ropeways, and there are

Above: *the Tanganyika
Tidal Wave*
Left: *beyond Orlando,
Busch Gardens is the
most visited theme park
in Florida*

slides, a sandpit, a carousel, watery activities and a children's theatre. The Living Dragons display features monitor lizards, Komodo dragons from Indonesia and giant iguanas.

Morocco At the entrance to the park, Morocco features attractive Moorish-style architecture and a clutch of souk-like stores selling North African craft items. Ice shows are held at the Moroccan Palace Theater and other diversions scheduled in the Marrakesh Theater.

A close encounter with the wildlife at Busch Gardens

Serengeti Plain transport
Elevated monorail (round-trip): Crown Colony. Sky Ride cable car: Crown Colony, Stanleyville. Serengeti Express Railroad: Egypt, Congo, Stanleyville

Nairobi First stop is Myombe Reserve: The Great Ape Domain, where the park's western lowland gorillas and chimpanzees nit-pick, snooze and occasionally stir themselves to get a better look at the humans. There are vampire bats, reptiles and snakes in Curiosity Caverns; baby birds and other residents in the Animal Nursery; a petting zoo, giant tortoises and elephants.

Serengeti Plain A 60-acre grassland enclosure reminiscent of the African veldt, inhabited by antelopes, giraffes, lions, rhinos and zebras. The park's Edge of Africa adventure promises a safari experience with close-up views of the animals, via a series of imaginatively designed enclosures, complete with a backing track of animal sounds and a range of evocative African smells running the olfactory gamut from camp fire to termite mound. Serengeti also boasts Rhino Valley, a rugged Land Rover Safari experience which packs thrills, spills and over 100 exotic African animals into it 8-minute journey.

Stanleyville Just the place to cool off with two great water rides: Tanganyika Tidal Wave (which soaks onlookers as well as passengers); and Stanley Falls Log Flume. There are reptile encounters at Snakes and More; the warthog and orangutan habitats; and a black spider monkey colony cavorting behind the fragrant and colourful Orchid Canyon. Guests can hop aboard the Serenget Express Railroad, shop for African crafts or enjoy family entertainments at the Stanleyville Theater.

Timbuktu At the heart of the park, Timbuktu's diversions include spooky special effects in R. L. Stine's Haunted Lighthouse; all-singing, all-dancing perfomances at Das Festhaus; thrills aboard the Scorpion roller-coaster and other fairground attractions, plus arcade games.

A Tour Around Blue Spring State Park

One of the prettiest state parks in Central Florida, Blue Spring is also famous for its winter season manatee population. The manatees usually visit between November and March, but the park is a great day out all year round, offering walking, boating and swimming opportunites, and it is a good place to enjoy a picnic (see panel ➤ 96).

From Orlando, take I-4 east (direction Daytona) to Exit 114. Follow US17-92 2½ miles south to Orange City. Blue Spring State Park is signposted off to the right at the junction with W French Avenue.

Lying along the wooded banks of the St Johns River, Florida's longest natural waterway, the park's namesake artesian spring is one of the largest in the US, producing around 100 million gallons of water a day. It really is blue, too. The turquoise pool at the spring head is a popular swimming hole for snorkelling, scuba-diving or just splashing around to cool off in the heat of the day.

During winter the warm spring waters, which gush forth at a constant 72°F, attract manatees from the cooler waters of the St Johns. From the waterside boardwalk there is a bird's-eye view of the manatees, and dozens of different fish and turtles swimming in the spring run; numerous waterbirds also congregate here. Canoes are available for rental and there are boat trips down the St Johns to nearby Hontoon Island State Park.

Follow the walking trail which starts near the Steamboat-era Thursby House.

Thursby House itself is perched on top of an ancient shell mound, left by Timucuan Indians. The trail leads through sand pine scrub, marshland and flatwood areas of the park.

Return to Orange City and take US17-92/I-4 back to Orlando.

A Jungle Cruise is an excellent way to enjoy Silver Springs' wildlife

Distance
60 miles round trip

Time
A 45-minute drive from Orlando. Allow at least 2 hours in the park

Start/end point
Orlando
✚ 46B2

Destination
Blue Spring State Park
✚ 46B3
✉ 2100 W French Avenue, Orange City
☎ (386) 775 3663
🕐 Daily 8AM–sunset
💲 Cheap

Lunch
Snack concessions and cold drinks available in the park

29B1

✉ 4777 W Irlo Bronson Highway/US192 (GM 12), Kissimmee; also at 6312 International Drive, Orlando

☎ (407) 396 6900

🕐 Daily 10AM–late

♿ Few

👖 Moderate

↔ Flying Tigers Warbird Restoration Museum (➤ 53), Jungleland Zoo (➤ 55)

✚ 46B1

✉ State Road 540 W, 4 miles east of Winter Haven (off US27, 22 miles south of I-4)

☎ (863) 324 2111 or 1-800 282 2123

🕐 Daily 5:30–9 (extended for special events)

Southern belles, in their antebellum dresses, adorn the grounds at Cypress Gardens

CONGO RIVER GOLF & EXPLORATION CO.

There is a choice of routes around this nifty mini-golf course and players are challenged to follow in the footsteps of 19th-century African explorers Henry Stanley and Dr David Livingstone. The obstacles are somewhat less dramatic and debilitating than those encountered by our heroes (there are no tsetse flies in Kissimmee), but the tropical layout is well provided with waterfalls, streams and mountainous boulders beneath the swaying palm trees. For those 'too pooped to putt', there are paddle boats and a games arcade. At the second location on International Drive, go-karts add to the fun.

CYPRESS GARDENS ✪✪✪

Florida's most sedate theme park, as well as its oldest, Cypress Gardens has until recently rather rested on its laurels, or rather its huge and colourful floral displays. The Botanical Gardens are still a treat, and there are flower festivals and impressive shows of massed blooms in the formal gardens throughout the year.

However, families can now enjoy visiting the Wings of Wonder butterfly conservatory, where it is fun to spot the hidden iguanas, turtles and tiny Asian doves. Birds of prey and reptile discovery shows are part of the Nature's Way animal habitat exhibit; and daily entertainment programmes feature concerts, shows, water-skiing spectaculars and nighttime laser light shows.

See also ➤ 18.

FANTASY OF FLIGHT ✪✪✪

Aviation historian, aerobatic pilot, designer and vintage aircraft restorer Kermit Weeks' second Florida air museum (the original is in Miami) showcases exhibits from Weeks' private aircraft collection alongside history displays and entertaining simulator rides.

Aviation buffs will find plenty to enjoy here down among the World War I fighters, 1920s barnstormers, Spitfires, Wildcats and Dauntless dive bombers from World War II – and even a battered Japanese Zero fighter, rescued from the treetops of New Guinea in the early 1990s. Aviation oddities are featured too, such as the Roadair flying automobile with retractable wings for highway driving, and an accurate replica of Charles A Lindbergh's *Spirit of St Louis*, which made the first transatlantic flight in 1927.

See also ➤ 19.

✚ 46A1
✉ SR-559, Polk City (I-4 West to Exit 44)
☎ (863) 984 3500
🕐 Daily 9–5

The Flying Tigers Warbird Restoration Museum preserves World War II airplanes in pristine flying condition

FLYING TIGERS WARBIRD RESTORATION MUSEUM ✪

From the slick presentation of Fantasy of Flight (above) to a real nuts-and-bolts operation. Working from a glory hole of a hangar-cum-workshop, surrounded by chunks of Flying Fortress, engines, propellors and wings, owner Tom Reilly and his team are the wizards of World War II aircraft restoration. Apparently irreparable bomber hulks are wheeled in and then resurrected to rise phoenix-like from the airstrip and go on to star in airshows around the country.

Every hour or so, a guided tour takes off around the museum and visitors are showered with information about the planes and their part in history. Practically everything can be touched – though woe betide any sticky fingers found smudging the fuselage of a fully restored Mustang. Several of the heftier restoration projects are lined up on the tarmac outside.

✚ 29B1
✉ 231 Hoagland Boulevard (GM 15.5), Kissimmee
☎ (407) 933 1942
🕐 Mon–Sat 9–5:30, Sun 9–5. Closed Chistmas and Thanksgiving
♿ Few
🍴 Moderate
↔ Congo River Golf & Exploration Co.(➤ 52), Jungleland Zoo (➤ 55)
❓ Take the controls of a T-6 WW II fighter trainer with Warbird Adventures, Inc. Reservations ☎ (407) 870 2295

53

A Tour Around Mount Dora

Distance
60 miles round trip

Time
A 50-minute drive from Orlando. Allow half a day to look around Mount Dora

Start/end point
Orlando
✚ 46B2

Destination
Mount Dora
✚ 46B3

Lunch
Windsor Rose English Tea Room (£)
✉ 144 W 4th Avenue
☎ (352) 735 2551

A pretty lakeshore town set amid gently rolling countryside and citrus groves, Mount Dora is renowned for its Victorian architecture and antiques shops.

From Orlando, take the Orange Blossom Trail/US441 north (direction Ocala) to Mount Dora, and follow signs for downtown.

Northern settlers first arrived on the shores of Lake Dora in the 1870s, and built their town on a low rise overlooking the eastern end of lake. The oldest surviving building in town is the 1883 Lakeside Inn, 100 Alexander Street, a short step away from the Chamber of Commerce.

At the Chamber of Commerce, 341 Alexander Street (☎ (352) 383 2165), pick up a driving map indicating a three-mile route around the pick of Mount Dora's historic homes and buildings.

The attractively restored downtown district is fun to explore. It is only a couple of blocks, but many of the old buildings house art galleries, speciality gift stores, tempting gourmet food emporiums and the popular antiques shops. Also in downtown is Mount Dora's most impressive historic home, the splendid Queen Anne-style Donnelly House. Ornately decorated with ironwork, a cupola, copious gables, balustrades, balconies and yards of gingerbread trim, it now serves as probably the daintiest Masonic Hall in the land. Near by, the town's former fire station and jail houses the small Royellou

Donnelly House, a Queen Anne-style confection in downtown Mount Dora

Museum, displaying local history exhibits. Down by the lake there is a nature trail in Palm Island Park; boats and bicycles are available for hire near the yacht club.

Return to Orlando on the US441 or SR46/I-4.

GREEN MEADOWS PETTING FARM

A great treat for small children, who can find the theme park experience and crowds a bit overwhelming. Here they can scamper about safely, clamber on tractors, collect acorns for the pigs and encounter all manner of other farmyard animals on the two-hour tours which allow them to meet and touch calves, lambs, kids, turkeys and fluffy yellow ducklings. Every child can milk a cow (if he or she wants to), and enjoy waggon rides and pony rides.

Free-ranging guineafowl, peacocks and chickens peck and preen around the attractive tree-shaded compound, which provides good protection from the hot sun, and toddlers or babies can be towed around in miniature farm trailers. Picnickers are welcome, there is a sunny grassed area and a sandpit and slides offer further fun.

JUNGLELAND ZOO

An old-fashioned zoo undergoing changes to develop a more naturalistic setting for its impressive collection of big cats and jungle-dwelling monkeys, lemurs and colourful birds. In fairness, most of the big cats, including imposing Bengal tigers, lions, leopards and cougars, have been hand-raised, so are used to their confined quarters and respond eagerly to their favourite keepers. The beautifully marked Diana monkeys, ruffled vervets and entertaining lemurs, too, are quite at home, and on-site comedian, Radcliffe the orangutan, made his name on the big screen as Clint Eastwood's sidekick, Clyde, in *Every Which Way But Loose*. There are giant porcupines and mongeese, capybaras (the world's largest rodent), chatty macaws, mynah birds, cockatoos and kookaburras. Buy a bag of seeds and grains to feed down the plastic chutes.

+ 46B2
✉ 1368 S Poinciana Boulevard, Kissimmee
☎ (407) 846 0770
◷ Daily 9:30–5:30 (last tour 4PM)
🍴 Snacks, sandwiches and cold drinks available (£)
♿ Few
👊 Moderate

+ 29B1
✉ 4580 W US192 (GM 14), Kissimmee
☎ (407) 396 1012
◷ Daily 9–6
♿ Good
👊 Moderate
↔ Congo River Golf & Exploration Co. (➤ 52), Flying Tigers Warbird Restoration Museum (➤ 53)

Above: *Green Meadows Petting Farm, a gentle alternative to alligators*

55

Food & Drink

Orlando knows a bit about mass catering. From sunrise to sunset and long into the night, the city's 4,300-plus restaurants, cafeterias, family diners and take-away operations aim to satisfy the hunger of a wildly divergent public, and on the whole they do pretty well.

Breakfast

For most visitors planning a long, busy day out and about sightseeing, the day begins with a traditional American breakfast, selected from a menu as long as your arm. Stockpile energy in the form of cereals, hot waffles or pancakes, served with bacon and maple syrup, eggs and hash browns, sweet fruit or bran muffins, toast or plain 'English muffins'. In general, hotel buffet breakfasts are reasonably priced, and several motels and suite hotels include a basic breakfast of cereal, muffins and pastries with coffee and fruit juice in the room price.

A typical American breakfast

Lunch

Lunch on the sightseeing trail often means alarming queues in the theme parks. The busiest time is between 12 and 2, so if you can manage to eat earlier or later it does make things easier. Guests who prefer a sit-down meal in a service restaurant at lunchtime should make reservations at the Guest Relations window when they arrive at the park. Otherwise there is usually a wide choice of eateries, from self-service cafeterias to hot dog stands, barbecue take-aways, sandwiches, burgers and ice creams, which can be eaten at outdoor seating areas.

Dinner

The evening meal is a very flexible affair in Orlando. Some restaurants start serving at 4PM to cater for those who have missed out on lunch or determined budget eaters who make the best of 'early bird specials', discounted meals offered before the restaurants really begin to fill up at around 6:30–7.

The main non-Walt Disney World Resort areas –

Florida Specialities

Florida's two main food groups are commonly known as 'surf 'n' turf' – that's seafood and beef. There are dozens of seafood restaurants in Orlando serving fresh fish, crab, lobster, shrimp and other delicacies. Steak houses and barbecue restaurants also do a roaring trade, and there is plenty of Southern-style Cajun or Creole influence in dishes, such as tasty blackened chicken or fish coated in spices and cooked over the grill.

Above: *traditional ribs*

International Drive and Kissimmee – are well provided with inexpensive family restaurants and fast food chains, as well as medium-price range steak houses, American, Chinese, Italian and Mexican eateries. For something more up-market, look to the top hotels, such as the Peabody Orlando, for a chance to dress up and enjoy a gourmet meal in notably elegant surroundings.

Medium-price bracket and expensive hotels generally provide a choice of dining options, and this is certainly true of the Walt Disney World Resort complexes. Restaurants serving up a selection of walking, talking oversized Disney characters along with their menu are a favourite with children, but do remember to book ahead to avoid disappointment (➤ 97 panel).

Drinking

Sightseeing is thirsty work in Orlando, and several rounds of soft drinks for the whole family at theme park or hotel prices can prove an expensive business. If you are on a budget, it is a good idea to stock up on bottled water, fruit juices or multi-packs of canned soft drinks at a supermarket. To buy or consume alcohol legally in the state of Florida, customers must be 21 or over.

Delicious, freshly squeezed fruit juice – essential on a hot day

A Tour Around Merritt Island National Wildlife Refuge

Distance
100 miles round trip; 120 miles as part of a day trip including Kennedy Space Center

Time
A 1¼ hour drive from Orlando; allow 40 minutes for the Black Point Wildlife Drive

Start/end point
Orlando
✚ 46B2

Destination
Merritt Island National Wildlife Refuge ☎ (321) 861 0667)
✚ 47D2

Lunch
Take a picnic or eat at the Kennedy Space Center – restaurants, cafés, snack concessions (£–££)

In clear sight of the Kennedy Space Center's looming Vehicle Assembly Building (VAB), Merritt Island National Wildlife Refuge occupies 220 square miles of marshland wilderness harbouring some 300 species of birds and dozens of other types of wildlife.

Take the Bee Line Expressway/SR528 toll road east from Orlando to SR407 north. Follow signs for the Kennedy Space Center onto SR405. At US1, turn left (north) and drive through Titusville. At the junction with SR406, turn right, cross the Indian River, and continue to the entrance to the Black Point Wildlife Drive on the left.

The northern portion of Merritt Island is a rare natural habitat preserve spanning fresh- and salt-water lagoons, mangrove islands, oak hardwood hammocks and palmetto-covered sand dunes, providing food and breeding grounds for an enormous variety of native Floridian wildlife. Endangered species such as manatees, wood storks and bald eagles live here, and sea turtles come ashore to lay their eggs on the Canaveral National Seashore during summer.

Follow the seven-mile Black Point Wildlife Drive.

At Stop 1, a viewfinder points out bald eagles' nests; at Stop 5, hundreds of wading birds can be seen feeding on the mud flats at low tide; and the

This nature conservation area's habitats range from pocket-sized freshwater lagoons to vast saltwater estuaries

five-mile Cruickshank Trail, a circular walk from Stop 8, has an observation tower just a few minutes' walk from the parking area.

Return on SR406, then turn right on SR402 for the Visitor Center.

The Center provides more information about the Refuge, and a further choice of walking trails.

KENNEDY SPACE CENTER   ❂❂❂

The Kennedy Space Center offers a unique opportunity for the public to learn about the people and machines behind the US space programme. A visit comprises a number of elements, including narrated bus tours of the historic Cape Canaveral Air Station facility and the unmissable Kennedy Space Center tour, which includes a photo stop in clear sight of the landmark Launch Complex 39, and the giant Vehicle Assembly Building, where the shuttles are prepared. Visitors can stop off as long as they like at the state-of-the-art Apollo/Saturn V Center with its excellent Apollo 8 launch experience, and a complete 363-foot-long Saturn V rocket on display. There is also a stop at the International Space Station Center.

Back at the main Visitor Complex, IMAX theatres present a variety of space themed programmes, of which the earth-shaking launch close-up *The Dream is Alive* is still the best. Earthlings can wander around towering exhibits in the Rocket Garden, clamber aboard a full-size shuttle replica and discover a wealth of artefacts, from space suits and astronaut food to space capsules, catch live show programmes and meet real astronauts face-to-face..

See also ➤ 20.

✚ 47D2
✉ SR405, Merritt Island (Bee Line Expressway/SR528 toll road east from Orlando to SR407 north, and follow signs)
☎ (321) 449 444 or (321) 454 4198 TDD
🕐 Daily 9–dusk
💲 Expensive
❓ Check schedules for the occasional Cape Canaveral: Then and Now tours

Historic spacecraft in the Rocket Park

Did you know ?

French science fiction writer Jules Verne predicted Florida's space age future almost a century before NASA arrived on the scene. In his novel From Earth to the Moon, *published in 1863, Verne described 'Florida...shaken to its very depths' by the blast-off of a rocket called* Columbiad, *a name strangely similar to the Columbia orbiter launched in 1981.*

➕ 46B2

Silver Spurs Rodeo
☎ For information call (407) 677 6336

Kissimmee Sports Arena
✉ 958 S Hoagland Boulevard
☎ (407) 933 0020
🕐 Fri 8PM–10PM

Old Town Kissimmee
✉ 5770 W Irlo Bronson Memorial Highway/US192 (GM 9.5), Kissimmee
☎ (407) 396 4888 or 1-800 843 4202
🕐 10AM–11PM
🍴 Fast food, snacks, several restaurants (£–££)
♿ Few
🆓 Free
↔ Water Mania (► 66)

Above: *Kissimmee, a popular vacation base south of Orlando, and a few minutes from Walt Disney World Resort*

KISSIMMEE ✪

Recent recipient of a $29-million face lift, Kissimmee's main drag stretches for miles along the US192 east–west cross route, either side of I-4. Its seamless run of local attractions and small shopping centres, chain restaurants and low-rise hotels has been newly landscaped and made more visitor-friendly with pavements and pedestrian access, transportation links and even bike racks. The quiet downtown district, at the junction with Orange Blossom Trail, has been restored.

Kissimmee is an attractive location for budget travellers. This is the place to find reasonably priced accommodation close to Walt Disney World Resort, and most hotels offer a free shuttle to the Disney parks. Inexpensive family restaurants are the order of the day along US192, and there are supermarkets for self-catering holidaymakers and plenty of family attractions close by. To help visitors find their way around US192, the city has erected a number of Guide-Markers (GM) along the highway. These are used in this guide to locate the various attractions.

A recreated turn-of-the-century Main Street, the **Old Town Kissimmee** open-air mall, provides an entertaining mixture of shops and half-a-dozen fairground rides, including the landmark Ferris wheel on the south side of Irlo Bronson Memorial Highway/US192. On Fridays and Saturdays a classic car parade is held here in the evening.

One of the top rodeo events on the professional Rodeo Cowboys Association southeastern circuit, the **Silver Spurs Rodeo**, takes place at Kissimmee biennially in February and October, and weekly demonstrations of calf-roping, bareback riding, steer wrestling and other skills take place at the **Kissimmee Sports Arena** on Fridays.

See also Flying Tigers Warbird Restoration Museum (► 53), Jungleland Zoo (► 55), Water Mania (► 66).

LAKE TOHOPEKALIGA

A short step from downtown Kissimmee, Lake Toho (as it is commonly known) offers an idyllic escape from the crowds. The 13-mile-long lake covers around 2,700 acres, with several islands in the middle where Seminole Indians once built forts. The bass fishing is excellent, and there is great birdwatching, with more than 120 species of birds living around the lake or visiting – like the winter population of white freshwater pelicans, who fly 2,000 miles south to escape the chilly northern temperatures.

The 30-foot *Eagle Ray* excursion boat takes passengers out on the lake from Big Toho Marina. Call **Aquatic Wonders Boat Tours** in advance and arrange for a half-day bass fishing trip with a knowledgeable guide, or a two-hour nature safari with a chance to see bald eagles, osprey, snail kites and more.

46B2

Aquatic Wonders Boat Tours

- ✉ 101 Lakeshore Boulevard
- ☎ (407) 846 2814
- 🕐 Daily 9–6 by reservation
- 💰 Expensive

LAKE WALES

A quiet country town south of Orlando, Lake Wales is famous for the **Black Hills Passion Play**, an annual event since 1953, which comes here in February and runs to mid-April, including Easter Sunday. The story of Christ's last days on earth is played in an amphitheatre surrounded by orange groves, and draws considerable crowds.

The **Lake Wales Museum and Cultural Center**, housed in a former railroad depot on the main street, features local history displays and railroad memorabilia. The other local attraction is Spook Hill, more correctly known as North Wales Drive. Visitors who drive to the bottom of the hill and put their vehicle in neutral at the white line will find that they appear to roll uphill.

46B1

Black Hills Passion Play

- ✉ Amphitheatre (south of Lake Wales)
- ☎ Schedules and reservations: (863) 676 1495 or 1-800 622 8383

Lake Wales Museum and Cultural Center

- ✉ 325 S Scenic Highway (Alt 27), Lake Wales
- ☎ (863) 678 4209
- 🕐 Mon–Fri 9–5, Sat 10–4
- ♿ Few
- 💰 Cheap
- 🔁 Bok Tower Gardens (➤ 47)

A beautiful Carolina wood duck, one of the many birds enjoying the waters of Lake Tohopekaliga

A Tour Around Ocala National Forest

Distance
95 miles round trip

Time
1¼ hour drive from Orlando.
Spend the full day in the
Forest, or also plan to visit
Silver Springs (➤ 22, 63)

Start/end point
Orlando
➕ 46B2

Destination
Ocala National Forest
➕ 46A4

Lunch
Take a picnic, or there are
snack concessions at
Recreation Areas within the
Forest (£)

*Friendly Ocala is famed
for its horses*

Within the boundaries of this 366,000-acre woodland preserve, the world's largest sand pine forest rolls back from the banks of the St Johns River, sprinkled with nearly 1,000 lakes and criss-crossed by miles of walking trails. Hikers will find peace and quiet along the numerous woodland paths. Other popular pastimes include paddling one of the beautiful canoe trails and fishing on Lake Dorr.

Take the Orange Blossom Trail/US441 north from Orlando to the SR19 exit at Eustis. Follow SR19 north for 11 miles to the Visitor Center at Lake Dorr; the main Ocala National Forest Visitor Center is on SR40, 12 miles east of Ocala.

Stop off at the Visitor Center for a free map and browse among the leaflets giving information about hiking trails and short walks. The Center can also supply details of fishing, canoeing and boating locations scattered around the forest. Ocala National Forest is at the heart of Central Florida's Big Scrub country, one of the few places Florida black bears still inhabit. It is also an important native habitat preserve for deer, wild turkeys, eagles and owls. Wading birds are at home here too, easily spotted from boardwalk trails or around the lakes.

Head for Juniper Springs Recreation Area at the head of the seven-mile Juniper Creek canoe run.

This is a favourite spot, where canoe reservations can be made in advance (☎ (352) 625 2808). Other recreation areas, such as Alexander Spring and Lake Dorr, offer swimming, picnicking and boat hire.

Return to Orlando along the SR40, SR19 and US441.

REPTILE WORLD SERPENTARIUM ✪

Rather off the beaten track, east of St Cloud, this no-frills serpentarium's main mission is research, and the collection and distribution of snake venoms. There are cobra and viper venom-gathering programmes three times a day (at 11, 2 and 5), and meticulous notes cover each snake display. Discover the secrets of the rattlesnake's tail, learn how to distinguish the non-venomous scarlet king snake from the poisonous eastern coral snake (same black, red and yellow colouring in subtly different proportions), and contemplate the world's largest snake species, the reticulated python and the massive green anaconda, known to snack on crocodiles in its native South America.

✚ 46C2
✉ 5705 E Irlo Bronson Memorial Highway/US192, 4 miles east of St Cloud
☎ (407) 892 6905
🕐 Tue–Sun 9–5:30. Closed Mon, Thanksgiving and Christmas
♿ Few
👋 Cheap

SILVER SPRINGS ✪✪✪

A Central Florida sightseeing destination since the 1870s, Silver Springs has augmented its natural attractions with a host of rides, shows and other essential modern-day theme park ingredients.

Alongside the ever-popular boat trips and jeep rides, favourite shows include the Alligator and Crocodile Encounter, which showcases 13 species of crocodilians and a rare white alligator, and Reptiles of the World, starring one of the alligator's few natural enemies, a 110lb snapping turtle.

Swimming is permitted in the spring only during July, but for hot summer days the **Wild Waters** water park is conveniently located next door.

See also ► 22.

✚ 46A4
✉ SR40, 1 mile east of Ocala (72 miles northwest of Orlando)
☎ (352) 236 2121 or 1-800 234 7458
🕐 Daily 9–5:30 (extended summer and hols)
🍴 The Deli (£); Springside Pizzeria (£); Springside Restaurant (£–££); Swampy's Smokehouse Buffet (£–££); snack stops, ice creams and cold drinks stalls (£)
♿ Good
👋 Very expensive; no extra charge for concerts
↔ Ocala National Forest (► 62)

Wild Waters
✉ Adjacent to Silver Springs on SR40
☎ (352) 236 2121 or 1-800 234 7458
🕐 Mar–Oct daily 10–7, extended in summer
👋 Expensive

A Silver Springs resident: a passing racoon gives a friendly wave

A Tour Around Wekiwa Springs State Park & Wekiwa River

Distance
36-mile round trip to Wekiwa Springs

Time
Orlando to Wekiwa Springs: 30 minutes

Start/end point
Orlando
46B2

Destination
Wekiwa Springs State Park
46B3
1800 Wekiwa Circle, Apopka
(407) 884 2008
Daily 8–sunset Cheap

Lunch
Take a picnic; snacks and cold drinks are available in the park

The Wekiwa River is one of Central florida's prettiest natural waterways. An unspoilt tributary of the St Johns, it flows on a lazy 15-mile journey north and east before emptying intothe main river near Sanford. The river borders the western edge of Seminole County, in an area known as the Central Florida Everglades. Just 344 square miles in total, Seminole County can boast some 2,000 freshwater lakes and rivers and offers numerous outdoor activities including walking, birdwatching, fishing and messing about in boats from gentle backwater canoe trips to airboat rides on alligator-infested Lake Jesup. The Wekiwa's headwaters rise in Wekiwa Springs State park.

Take I–4 eastbound from orlando to Exit 94. Head west on SR434, and look for the right turn on to Wekiwa Springs Road, which leads straight to the park.

This is a lovely woodland park with plenty of shade and over 13 miles of hiking trails. The main loop trail visits native habitat areas ranging from dry sand ridges to low, swampy areas close to the Rock Springs Run (be prepared for mosquitoes in summer); there are several shorter trails as well. Swimming is permitted in the refreshing main spring ('Wekiwa' means 'spring of water' in Creek Indian), and canoes are available for rental.

For those interested in a guided kayak tour, contact River Quest Kayaks, 4043 S Hwy 17/92, Casselberry (407) 834 4040, who also provide canoe rentals and free demonstrations daily. Airboat rides into alligator territory can be arranged through Gator Ventures of Seminole, 2536 Black Hammock Fish Camp Road, Oviedo (407) 977 8325.

Take I-4 back to Orlando.

SPLENDID CHINA

⚫⚫⚫

A ride-free zone where small is beautiful, Splendid China is a theme park with a difference. The speciality here is miniaturisation: 60 famous Chinese natural and manmade landmarks are rendered in unbelievable detail at a fraction of their original size.

Perhaps the most ambitious project is the Great Wall of China, rolling sinuously up hill and down dale for half-a-mile, dividing, as it was designed to do in the 3rd century BC, the civilised Middle Kingdom from the northern Barbarians (represented by a Mongolian Yurt exhibit). Another notably lavish undertaking is the Imperial Palace/Forbidden City complex.

Take a break from the sightseeing trail for the shows, and lunch Chinese-style at one of the on-site restaurants. The Chinatown marketplace, at the entrance to the park, has stalls and shops selling T-shirts and Chinese silk robes, embroidery, jewellery, wind chimes and fortune cookies.

See also ► 23.

* 🞢 29A1
* ✉ 3000 Spendid China Boulevard/GM 4.5, Kissimmee (3 miles west of I-4/Exit 25-B)
* ☎ (407) 396 7111 or 1-800 244 6226
* 🕐 Daily 9:30–7 (extended summer and hols)
* 🍴 The Great Wall Terrace (£–££); Wind and Rain Court (£–££); Pagoda Garden (£); Seven Flavours (£); Hong Kong Seafood Restaurant (£££)
* ♿ Very good
* 👆 Very expensive
* ↔ A World of Orchids (► 46)

US ASTRONAUT HALL OF FAME

⚫⚫

Recently amalgamated with the neighbouring Kennedy Space Center, this is a popular stop with children, who enjoy the hands-on approach. There's lots of interactive fun here, along with space hardware exhibits from the Mercury and Gemini programmes and entertaining rides such as Shuttle to Tomorrow, a flight into the future aboard a full-scale mock-up of a 120-foot orbiter. Potential astronauts get to put themselves to the test with the G-Force Trainer, and another favourite attraction is the stomach-churning 3D-360° flight simulator ride – which is pretty good fun to watch as well.

* 🞢 47D2
* ✉ 6225 Vectorspace Boulevard/SR405, Titusville
* ☎ (321) 269 6100
* 🕐 Daily 9–5 (extended summer and hols)
* 🍴 Cosmic Cafe (£)
* ♿ Good 👆 Moderate
* ↔ Kennedy Space Center (► 20, 59), Merritt Island Wildlife Refuge (► 58)

An astronauts' showcase

WATER MANIA ✪

Kissimmee's very own spash zone, this is the place to cool off in the height of summer or just enjoy a family day out. The 36-acre site features wave pools, lagoons, small children's watery fun areas and lazy inner tube rides on Cruisin' Creek. Thrill-seekers can shoot the body-surfing-style Wipe Out ride, the Screamer, the Double Berzerker, Twin Tornados, the blacked-out Abyss and curvaceous Anaconda. On a drier note, there are arcade games, mini-golf, beach volleyball and basketball, and picnic facilities.

WINTER PARK ✪✪✪

A smart northern suburb of Orlando, Winter Park boasts a brace of fine art museums, an attractive shopping district and scenic boat trips on a chain of small lakes edged by millionaires' mansions. The town was originally laid out as a genteel winter resort for wealthy New Englanders in the 1880s. Its main street, Park Avenue, is lined with boutiques and art galleries, shops selling exclusive interior design knick-knacks and chic restaurants. On Saturdays, the local Farmers' Market, on New England Avenue, is a favourite stop for fruit and vegetable shopping and fresh-baked goods, or just browsing among the colourful stalls.

Morse Museum of American Art Pride of place goes to the gallery's world-famous collection of Tiffany glass, much of it salvaged from Laurelton Hall, Louis Comfort Tiffany's Long Island home, which burned down in 1957. Many of Tiffany's own favourite pieces are on display, such as the glorious Rose Window. There are earthy fruit and vegetable stained-glass still lifes, others depicting magnolia blooms and elegant wisteria lampshades. Further collections cover ceramics, furniture and metalwork, and Tiffany's contemporaries also get a look in, with glassware from René Lalique and Emile Galle, paintings by Maxfield Parrish, and contributions from Frank Lloyd Wright.

Rollins College and Cornell Fine Arts Museum Florida's oldest college, established in 1885, Rollins' original campus buildings were constructed in fashionable Spanish-Mediterranean style on a pretty campus overlooking Lake Virginia. Near the entrance to the campus, the Walk of Fame features more than 400 stepping stones gathered from the birthplaces and homes of famous people, from Mary, Queen of Scots and Benjamin Franklin to Buffalo Bill. There is an attractive college chapel and theatre linked by a loggia, and the small but perfectly formed Cornell Fine Arts Museum housing notable collections of European Old Master paintings, 19th- and 20th-century American art, Indian artefacts and decorative arts (displayed on a rotating basis).

Opposite: splashtacular fun at Water Mania

Cornell Fine Arts Museum
- ✉ Rollins College, Holt Avenue, Winter Park
- ☎ (407) 646 2526
- 🕐 Tue–Fri 10–5, Sat–Sun 1–5. Closed Mon
- ♿ Good
- 🎫 Free

Outstanding works of art can be found at the Cornell

Scenic Boat Tours A chain of six little freshwater lakes around Winter Park is linked by narrow, leafy canals. The canals were once used to transport logs, but now facilitate the movement of small boats and allow scenic boat trips to putter from Lake Osceola down to Lake Virginia and up to Lake Maitland. The tours last about an hour and offer a prime view of Winter Park's most exclusive lake frontage - the grandest homes overlook Lake Maitland. Waterbirds are easy to spot and there is the occasional glimpse of an alligator.

Scenic Boat Tours
- ✉ 312 E Morse Boulevard, Winter Park
- ☎ (407) 644 4056
- 🕐 Daily 10–4 on the hour, except Christmas
- ♿ Few
- 🎫 Moderate

67

In the Know

If you only have a short time to visit Orlando, or would like to get a flavour of the region, here are some ideas:

10
Ways To Be A Local

Dress comfortably and coolly. Floridians are also casual dressers and jackets and ties for men are rarely required.
Game on Check out Orlando's action-packed sporting scene from orlando Magic's basketball skills to baseball spring training (➤ 112).
Gator wrestling is best left to the professionals. Instead, watch a demonstration at Gatorland (➤ 32).
Go fishing – this is how the locals relax, leaving the theme parks to visitors.
'Have a nice day' is not just an automatic platitude in Orlando: people really mean it.
Sample grits, the breakfast porridge of the Southern US, made from roughly ground boiled corn mixed with butter.
Tipping is a way of life here, not just in bars and restaurants, but for just about any kind of service from valet parking to shuttle bus drivers.
Tolls are payable on the Bee Line Expressway and Florida Turnpike, so keep some small change accessible in the car.
Turn right on red at traffic lights in Florida unless a stop sign dictates otherwise – but look out for other road-users and pedestrians.
Western wear is high fashion during Kissimmee's famous rodeo events. Snap up a pair of alligator-skin boots (➤ 107).

10
Good Places To Cool Off

Blizzard Beach (➤ 88).
Blue Spring (➤ 51).
Canaveral National Seashore offers 30 miles of unspoilt seashore and beaches stretching north of the Kennedy Space Center (➤ 58).
Cocoa Beach is one of Florida's famous 'party' beaches on the Atlantic Coast, an hour's drive down the Bee Line Expressway/SR528.
River Country (➤ 90).
Tanganyika Tidal Wave at Busch Gardens (➤ 50).
Typhoon Lagoon (➤ 90).
Water Mania (➤ 66).
Wekiwa Springs (➤ 64).
Wet 'n Wild (➤ 43).

10
Best Theme Park Restaurants

To make advance reservations, contact Guest Relations on entering the park.
Aloha Polynesian Luau
✉ SeaWorld Orlando
☎ (407) 363 2559.
Dinner-only South Seas feast and entertainment (call ahead to make

'Have a nice day'

reservations).

Brown Derby ✉ Disney-MGM Studios, Walt Disney World ☎ (407) 939 3463. Cool and clubby replica of Hollywood moguls' meeting place. Pasta, steaks, Cobb salad.

Buccaneer Smokehouse ✉ SeaWorld Orlando ☎ (407) 351 3600. Mesquite-grilled barbecued ribs, chicken and beef.

Chefs de France ✉ Epcot, Walt Disney World ☎ (407) 939 3463. Elegant Disney outpost for French *nouvelle cuisine*.

Coral Reef ✉ Epcot, Walt Disney World ☎ (407) 939 3463. First-class seafood and a stunning view of the coral reef exhibition.

Crown Colony ✉ Busch Gardens, Tampa ☎ (813) 987 5600. Family restaurant overlooking the animals of the Serengeti Plain exhibit. Chicken dinners, fresh seafood, sandwiches.

Hard Rock Café ✉ Universal Studios, CityWalk, Orlando ☎ (407) 351 7625. Big fun, big name rock memorabilia and big burgers.

Hong Kong Seafood Restaurant ✉ Splendid China, Kissimmee ☎ (407) 397 8800. Chinese cuisine and familiar favourites, from Cantonese crispy shrimp to Hong Kong beef fillet.

Liberty Tree Tavern ✉ Magic Kingdom, Walt Disney World ☎ (407) 939 3463. All-American home-style cooking in a re-created colonial inn. Turkey dinners, Cape Cod pasta, pot roast.

Lombard's Landing ✉ Universal Studios Florida, Orlando ☎ (407) 224 6401. Seafood specialities, pasta and steaks, plus waterfront dining in the re-created San Francisco district.

10
Top Golf Courses

Arnold Palmer Golf Academy ✉ 9000 Bay Hill Boulevard, Orlando ☎ (407) 876 5362.

Black Bear Golf Club ✉ 24505 Calusa Boulevard, Eustis ☎ (352) 357 4732 or 1-800 423 2718.

Celebration Golf Club ✉ 701 Golf Park Drive, Celebration ☎ (407) 566 4653.

Disney's 99 Holes of Golf ✉ Walt Disney World Resort, Lake Buena Vista ☎ (407) 824 4321.

Faldo Golf Institute by Marriott 12001 Avenida Verde, Orlando ☎ (407) 238 7677

Grand Cypress ✉ Grand Cypress Resort, North Jacaranda, Orlando ☎ (407) 239 1904.

MetroWest Golf Club ✉ 2100 S Hiawassee Road, Orlando ☎ (407) 299 1099.

Orange County National Golf Center ✉ 16301 Phil Ritson Way, Winter Garden ☎ (407) 656 2626 or 1-888 PAR 3672

Stoneybrook Golf Club ✉ 2900 Northampton Avenue, Orlando ☎ (407) 384 6888.

Timacuan Golf & Country Club ✉ 550 Timacuan Boulevard, Lake Mary ☎ (407) 321 0010.

10
Free Attractions

Audubon's Center for Birds of Prey ✉ 1101 Audubon Way, Maitland ☎ (407) 644 0190. Aviaries housing birds of prey, including eagles, owls and hawks.

Bradlee-McIntyre House ✉ 130 W Warren Avenue (at CR427), Longwood ☎ (407) 332 0225. Orange County's only Victorian cottage.

Cornell Fine Arts Museum ✉ Rollins College, Winter Park ☎ (407) 646 2526. Exhibitions of old masters and contemporary fine arts (► 67).

Fort Christmas Park ✉ 1300 Fort Christmas Road, Christmas ☎ (407) 568 4149. Replica fort, pioneer homes and Seminole War exhibits.

Lake Eola Park ✉ Eola Drive, Orlando ☎ (407) 246 2827. Downtown's lakeside park with picnicking areas, children's playground and boat rentals.

Kraft Azalea Gardens ✉ Alabama Drive, Winter Park. Azaleas, subtropical plants and cypress trees on shore of Lake Maitland.

Lakeridge Winery & Vineyards ✉ 19239 N US27, Clermont ☎ (352) 394 8627 or 1-800 768 9463. Guided tours and tastings.

Maitland Historical Museum & Telephone Museum ✉ 221 W Packwood Avenue, Maitland ☎ (407) 644 2451. Artefacts, photos and memorabilia.

West Orange Trail ✉ Winter Garden ☎ (407) 877 0600. A 4½-mile trail for walkers, cyclists and skaters (bike and skate rental available).

Zora Neale Hurston National Museum of Fine Arts ✉ 227 E Kennedy Boulevard, Eatonville ☎ (407) 647 3307. Exhibits by artists of African descent in Zora Neale Hurston's (► 14) home town.

Walt Disney World Resort

Walt Disney World Resort is the apogee of the Disney phenomenon. It is a fairytale fiefdom, where litter and spoiltsports are banned and Cinderella Castle pops out of the storybook and into 3-D reality. Disney's appeal is universal. It makes nonsense of age and cultural barriers uniting people from all walks of life in the pursuit of good, clean family fun and escapist fantasy. Teams of 'imagineers' have resurrected everybody's favourite characters, then added the latest screen stars, state-of-the-art rides, shows and even gently educational exhibits spread over the theme parks, water parks and entertainment districts.

Some find it all too perfect, and Disney's reputation for ruthless efficiency leads to charges of blandness. However, the prime objective here is family entertainment and that, even the most grudging cynic has to admit, Disney delivers in abundance.

> *'I have never called this art. It's show business, and I am a showman.'*

WALTER ELIAS DISNEY,
(1901–66)

———————•———————

Photograph: © Disney

Left: *fun on Big Thunder Mountain Railroad*

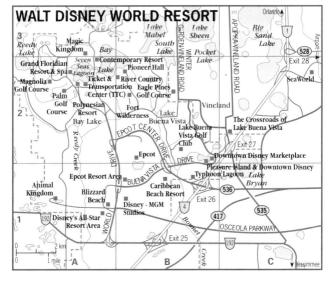

WALT DISNEY WORLD RESORT

🗝 29A1 (and above)

✉ Walt Disney World
Resort, Lake Buena Vista
(I-4/Exits 25-B and 26-B,
south of Orlando)

☎ (407) 824 4321

🕐 Check current schedules

🍴 Each park offers a wide
choice of dining options
open for breakfast, lunch,
dinner, and snacks
throughout the day.
Priority seating (bookings
service at Guest
Relations) is advised for
table service restaurants
(££–£££)

🚌 Free shuttle bus services
from many Orlando/
Kissimmee hotels

♿ Excellent

💰 Very expensive. Note that
children of 10 and over
qualify for adult tickets;
children's tickets are for
ages 3–9; under 3 free.

Walt Disney World Resort

The cooler winter months are the most comfortable time to visit Walt Disney World Resort, and the crowds are definitely less pressing either side of the Christmas rush (January until mid-February, and mid-September until Christmas, with the exception of the busy Thanksgiving holiday). However, expect to queue whenever you go, and be well prepared with loose, comfy clothing, sturdy footwear and sunblock.

Ticket options: Daily One Park/One Day admission tickets are valid for one park only on the stated day. For longer stay guests, multi-day tickets offer flexibility and savings. There are **2-, 3-, 4- and 5-Day Park Hopper Plus Passes**, which cover a) unlimited admission to any combination of theme parks over the duration of the ticket, b) use of the WDW Resort transportation system, and c) choice of complimentary admission to Pleasure Island or Disney Quest. The **5-, 6- and 7-Day Park Hopper Plus Passes** cover a) and b) above, plus a choice of entries under category c), and the waterparks and Disney's Wide World of Sports. Unused days never expire and can be used on a future visit. Guests at certain properties can purchase the **Ultimate Park Hopper**, which provides admission to all Disney's WDW attractions. New 'After 2' tickets offer 1- or 2-day admission to any one theme park after 2PM.

FASTPASS Save time queuing for the most popular rides in all four Disney theme parks with the FASTPASS system. Simply pop your regular park ticket into the FASTPASS machine at the attractions offering the complimentary service and you will receive a designated return time with no need to queue. The FASTPASS allows a one-hour window from the time printed on the ticket during which you should present yourself at the FASTPASS entrance with your ticket and sail straight through. You can only have one FASTPASS running at any one time, i.e. you must have used (or exceeded the time allocation for) one FASTPASS before you can collect another. Attractions offering this service are indicated on Disney maps and in this guide by the letters (FP).

What to Expect The Disney parks provide a wide range of guest facilities, from baby strollers and lockers to banking and kennelling. A limited number of wheelchairs are available, and there are special arrangements for sight- and hearing-impaired visitors. Guest relations can also help with lost and found queries, camera rentals and free battery-charging.

Details of daily parades, showtimes and night-time fireworks and laser displays are printed in current park guides. Hotel, campground, show and ticket reservations can be made through Central Reservations (☎ 407/934 7639, fax (407) 354 1866). Dining reservations can be made up to 60 days in advance (☎ (407) 939 3463).

Main Street, U.S.A. in Magic Kingdom Park, leading up to Cinderella Castle

Photograph: © Disney

72A1

Osceola Parkway, Walt
Disney World Resort

(407) 824 4321

Check current schedules

Fascinating Facts

If you washed and dried one
load of laundry every day for
44 years, you would clean as
much as the Walt Disney
World Resort Laundry handles
in a single day.

Around 450,000 miles of
lawn are mown at Walt
Disney World Resort each
year: the equivalent of 18 trips
around the equator.

Enough Mouse Ear hats are
sold every year to cover the
head of every man, woman
and child in Pittsburgh.

*Coming face to face with
zebras and giraffes on a
safari*

DISNEY'S ANIMAL KINGDOM ✪✪✪

Walt Disney World Resort's fourth full scale theme park,
Disney's Animal Kingdom, focuses Disney's famous imagination and attention to detail on the natural world. The
500-acre site features five themed districts and boasts
more than 200 animal species showcased in impressively
re-created naturalistic habitats. Not content with the
wonders of the world about us, Disney has also gone for
the populist angle with DinoLand U.S.A., a fun celebration
of the dinosaur era. Amongst all the fun and games,
however, care has been taken to incorporate a worthy
conservationist message.

For the best chance of seeing the animals at their most
active, it really does pay off to arrive at Disney's Animal
Kingdom as early as possible in the day. From The Oasis
entry point, head for Safari Village and the footbridge links
to the other four districts. Then secure your first
FASTPASS (▶ 72).

Africa & Rafiki's Plant Watch African-styled Harambe
Village is the start point for two excellent big game viewing
opportunities. Kilimanjaro Safaris (FP) is Disney's Animal
Kingdom's unmissable ride, a Jeep journey deep into the

Did you know ?

More than 4 million plants, including 100,000 trees and 4 million grasses and new shrubs, were used to create the exotic and varied landscapes of Disney's Animal Kingdom, and there are more than 350 types of grass growing here. On a less realistic note, The Tree of Life has 103,000 hand-painted leaves.

More Fascinating Facts

Walt Disney World Resort has a daily population of 200,000 people.

More than 2,600 couples get married at Walt Disney World Resort every year.

If all the hot dogs and hamburgers consumed by Walt Disney World Resort guests each year were lined up end to end they would stretch from Orlando to Philadelphia.

Walt Disney World Resort generates 70 tons of waste every day, of which 35 tons is recycled on site.

re-created African veldt inhabited by lions, cheetahs, rhinos, giraffes, wildebeest, zebras and others. The ride is brought to a rather abrupt end by a rescue mission to save the elephants from poachers, but the Pangani Forest Exploration Trail allows a closer look at some of the safari animals, notably an underwater view of the hippos, plus an invitingly lush and misty gorilla habitat. Mosey on down to Harambe Station to catch the Wildlife Express miniature train ride, which wends its way past the 'backlot' animal quarters to Rafiki's Plant Watch. Here interactive exhibits

on endangered species are presented alongside picture windows viewing into the animal nursery, and veterinary suite.

Asia Exuberant rainforest-type foliage and colourful tropical flowers set the tone for the Maharaja Jungle Trek, a gentle stroll through elaborate Indian temple ruins to the tiger enclosure and exotic bird aviaries. After the trek, visit the Flights of Wonder birds of prey show, or down a cool drink in the leafy Siamang Viewing Area. Asia's action adventure is the Kali River Rapids (FP), a whitewater rafting ride that shoots beneath tunnels of overhanging bamboo, past giant boulders and a series of cooling water jets.

Camp Minnie-Mickey Set slightly apart from the main bustle, this district is a good place for families with young children to take a break. Camp Minnie-Mickey's character greeting areas field a full team of classic Disney figures from Mickey and Goofy to favourites from *The Jungle Book*. Pocahontas and Her Forest Friends is a cute child-oriented show with live animal performers; while the Festival of the Lion King is a real crowd-pleasing spectacular for all ages, featuring high-energy dance and acrobatic routines, fire-jugglers and stilt-walkers. And check schedules for Mickey's Jammin' Jungle Parade, which tootles through the camp every afternoon.

75

DinoLand U.S.A. Prehistory with a Disneyesque spin begins at the Olden Gate Bridge, a 40-foot Brachiosaurus skeleton marking the entrance to DinoLand U.S.A. First stop for kids is The Boneyard play area. Follow this with a visit to the Fossil Preparation Lab, where real life paleontologists undertake their research into dinosaur remains, while guests are dwarfed by the impressive collection of life-size casts taken from dinosaur skeletons in the Dinosaur Jubilee exhibition area. On the thrills front, there is rollercoaster action aboard Primeval Whirl! and the Dinosaur (FP) ride is a 'must', offering a time travel expedition back to the end of the dinosaur era. Dodge meteorite showers and ravening, blood-thirsty 'animatronic' dinosaurs in an attempt to bring back a dear little veggie dino for posterity. For light relief, check out the Tarzan Rocks! acrobatic rock music extravaganza or take a four-person dino vehicle for a gentle 'dino soar' with TriceraTop Spin.

Safari Village At the heart of Safari Village, The Tree of Life is the centrepiece and symbol of the park. The trunk, branches and root system of the 145-foot tall landmark have been carved with 325 animal images and around its vast bulk the Safari Village Trails meander past assorted enclosures for lemurs, kangaroos, capybaras and other small- to medium-sized animals. Beneath the roots, a subterranean theatre presents It's Tough to be a Bug (FP), an entertaining and imaginative 3-D look at life from a bug's perspective starring Flik and Hopper from *A Bug's Life*. (Some surprise effects could upset children scared of creepy-crawlies.)

72B1

Walt Disney World Resort

(407) 824 4321

DISNEY-MGM STUDIOS ✪✪

Disney-MGM Studios was Walt Disney World Resort's riposte to the news that Universal Studios were opening a rival theme park-cum-studio facility at Orlando in 1990. Disney squeezed in just ahead, opening in 1989, and have almost doubled the size of the original park, though it remains rather shorter on rides than its chief rival. However, there is plenty of Disney flair on display and constantly updated exhibits showcase popular new productions, and give a chance to watch Disney's skilled animators at work.

Backlot Tour After a visit to the splash tank and a chance to participate in a demonstration of special effects at sea, hop aboard a tram to cruise past the Star's Parking Lot, the world's largest working wardrobe department, and the props and special effects departments. There are a couple of surprises in store at Catastrophe Canyon before arriving at the American Film Institute Showcase for a display of prize props and film memorabilia.

The Great Movie Ride On Hollywood Boulevard a full-scale re-creation of Mann's Chinese Theater is the setting for this ambitious homage to movie classics. Audio-Animatronics® figures replace the great stars in famous screen scenes.

Honey, I Shrunk the Kids Movie Set An imaginative children's adventure play area featuring giant bugs, spider's web rope ladders, looming blades of grass and cooling water jets for welcome relief on a hot day.

Photograph: © Disney

Animators on The Disney-MGM Backlot Tour

Transport across WDW

WDW Resort buses (free to WDW Resort guests and multi-day pass holders) service the parks from the main Transportation and Ticket Center at Magic Kingdom; journeys take up to 90 mins

The sprawling WDW site is difficult to negotiate, although the complex road system is well-signposted. There are considerable distances between the various parks and resort hotels, which make a car useful, though not essential.

Thrills on the Rock 'n' Roller Coaster Starring Aerosmith

Indiana Jones® Epic Stunt Spectacular! (FP) Check schedules with the updated show times listed in the park's free giveaway map, and catch a performance of this explosive stunt show. 'Audience volunteers' get an opportunity to join in the fun.

Jim Henson's Muppet Vision 3-D (FP) Jim Henson's magnificent Muppets steal the show hands down. A terrific combination of big screen 70mm, 3-D film action, monster special effects and anarchic humour.

The Magic of Disney Animation A brief but illuminating insight into the world of animation which traces the long and painstaking road from a story idea to the finished product. Check out the original artworks in the animation gallery before the tour leads off through the production studios, where artists crouch over their drawing boards.

Rock 'n' Roller Coaster Starring Aerosmith (FP) A giant red electric guitar fronts this thrilling roller-coaster ride in the dark. After joining the heavy rock band Aerosmith at a studio session guests are invited on a limo race against time to reach the band's evening gig accompanied by a thumping soundtrack and some pretty hairy manoeuvres.

Sounds Dangerous Starring Drew Carey Seriously funny

Photograph: © Disney

man Drew Carey takes the lead in a spoof pilot for a new TV investigative show, *Undercover Live*, and explores the world of sound in a darkened theatre. Most of the action takes place in a total blackout as the audience's ears are assailed by a trip to the

barber and a swarm of killer bees amongst other weird and wonderful soundsational experiences.

Star Tours A bone-shaking intergalatic thrill ride on a runaway space ship. Wild simulator action, dazzling special effects. The pre-flight warnings aimed at pregnant women, heart condition sufferers and the faint-hearted should also deter anybody who has eaten recently.

Theater of the Stars In a setting reminiscent of the Hollywood Bowl, the 1,500-seat Theater of the Stars hosts musical spectaculars guaranteed to appeal to audiences of all ages. Other stage shows starring favourite Disney characters appear at the Backlot Theater. On Fridays and Saturdays, nightly in summer and at peak holiday periods, the Hollywood Hills Amphitheatre is the setting for the park's outstanding fireworks and nighttime show spectaculars which also draw their inspiration from Disney classics.

The Twilight Zone Tower of Terror™ (FP) A quiet stroll down Sunset Boulevard is soon interrupted by the shrieks of terrified passengers plummeting down the lift shaft of the spooky Hollywood Tower Hotel. Guests encounter various mysterious manifestations on the route to the top of the 199-foot building before a series of plunges.

Voyage of The Little Mermaid (FP) Beloved of little girls the world over, Ariel (The Little Mermaid of the title) gets the full theme park treatment as her story is retold with clever special effects, puppets, Audio-Animatronics, film clips and live performers.

Walt Disney – One Man's Dream Compiled as part of Disney's 100 Years of Magic Celebration!, this look at the theme park visionary's life and achievements features artefacts and previously unseen film footage.

Who Wants To Be A Millionaire – Play It! (FP) A chance for fans of the hit TV quiz to get a taste of the real thing in a meticulously recreated studio setting. Sadly no one wins a million, but there are prizes.

 72B2

✉ Epcot Center Drive, Walt
Disney World Resort

☎ (407) 824 4321

🕐 Check current schedules

*Epcot's trademark – the
silver Spaceship Earth
geosphere – is a time
machine in which you ride
from the past to the stars*

80

EPCOT ✪✪

Walt Disney's original plan to create a Utopian-style research community living on the Epcot (Experimental Prototype Community of Tomorrow) site never came to fruition, but his ideas have been adapted to provide a semi-educational showcase for new technology and sciences and a window on the world around us.

Epcot, twice the size of Magic Kingdom, is divided into two parts. In the shadow of a giant silver geosphere, the Future World pavilions house the scientific stuff, with displays focusing on transport, communications, health, energy, agriculture and oceanology. This sounds rather serious, but the Walt Disney Imagineers have added plenty of hands-on fun, rides and film shows. The second section of the park is World Showcase, a 1.3-mile promenade through 11 'villages', each representing the potted history, culture and architecture of a different nation.

FUTURE WORLD

Innoventions Tomorrow's technology today, as top companies preview the latest developments in science and technology in an interactive environment. The two Innoventions pavilions are packed with hands-on fun from virtual tag games with Mickey and Minnie to video challenges designed to test players' problem-solving skills and knowledge of a range of science, technology and environmental subjects. Guests can build a family homepage at the Web Site Construction Zone; check out the future of the automobile; and tour the 'smart home' of tomorrow, which includes a robot dog amongst its innovations.

Journey into Imagination with Figment A lacklustre presentation narrated by Monty Python stalwart Eric Idle, who shares the billing with a perky little dragon called Figment. The rides grinds through a series of colourful scenes purporting to represent an exploration of human imagination and depostits bemused passengers into the interactive ImageWorks area to experiment with their own images. Much more fun is the hugely entertaining Honey, I Shrunk the Audience (FP) 3-D show in the movie theatre.

The Land There are two deservedly popular attractions here, starting with Living with the Land (FP). This gentle boat ride journeys through various environments explaining how plants survive, then continues into a futuristic green-house world where some of the fresh produce served in Walt Disney World Resort restaurants is grown. This is quite a sight as you glide past citrus trees laden with giant 9-pound lemons (each capable of producing two pints of juice), and string gardens where cucumbers, eggplants and banks of lettuces grow vertically. Guests who would like a closer look at The Land's experimental greenhouses should sign up for **Behind The Seeds**, a behind-the-scenes guided walk tour.

On the upper level of the pavilion, the Circle of Life Theater presents an excellent eco-conscious film show starring characters from *The Lion King*: Simba the Lion King turns Simba-the-Educator and talks Pumbaa and Timon out of polluting Africa with the Hakuna Matata Electric Disco Holiday Resort. Pretty hard-hitting stuff for Orlando.

The Living Seas This 6-million-gallon salt water marine exhibit is a favourite stop. The centrepiece is an amazing man-made coral reef inhabited by 2,000 colourful and curious tropical fish. A short introductory film prefaces the descent to Seabase Alpha for a ride through the aquarium to the observation levels for views of sharks, bottlenose dolphins and sea turtles. Manatees, Florida's endangered prehistoric sea cows, also feature.

Recommended Epcot Restaurants

🍽 Future World: Coral Reef, The Living Seas
World Showcase: Chefs de France, France; L'Originale Alfredo di Roma, Italy; Nine Dragons, China; Mitsukoshi Teppan Yaki Dining Room, Japan

❓ Make lunch or dinner reservations at Guest Relations on entering park

Behind The Seeds

✉ Reservations at Green Thumb gift store, The Land pavilion

🕐 Tours (1 hour) depart every hour 10:30–4:40

✋ Moderate additional charge

A boat glides by the fabulous Morocco Pavilion

Spaceship Earth An entertaining ride through the history of communication inside the landmark 180-foot-high aluminium geosphere. Dioramas illustrate man's progress from cave paintings to a nifty neon journey down the Information Superhighway. Then passengers disembark into the AT&T Global Neighborhood and its diverting assortment of hands-on games with a futuristic flavour.

Test Track (FP) The longest and fastest ride ever created by Walt Disney Imagineers features road test automobile action. Take to the track for a tyre-squealing, three-storey ascent and assorted high-speed manoeuvres in the dark.

Universe of Energy Arguably the best ride in the park, Ellen's Energy Adventure, a humorous romp back to the dinosaur era, stars comedian Ellen DeGeneres in her own nightmare: an episode of the game show *Jeopardy* in which all the questions relate to energy. Cue Bill Nye, the Science Guy, who whisks Ellen (and the audience) off to a land of impressive Audio-Animatronic dinosaurs for a lesson on fossil fuels. A CircleVision 360° film covers modern energy sources and *Jeopardy* is a piece of cake,

Wonders of Life Humankind comes under the microscope in this pavilion, home to the entertaining Cranium Command show, taking a look at the random workings of a

82

12-year-old boy's brain. The bumpy Body Wars thrill ride plunges through the human anatomy. Meanwhile, The Making of Me handles human reproduction (parental discretion advised), and the AnaComical Players improvise skits on health issues.

WORLD SHOWCASE

The American Adventure The centrepiece of the World Showcase villages presents a 30-minute dramatised history of America.

Canada Feast the eyes on the CircleVision 360° *O Canada!* film and stock up on maple leaf motifs at a Rockies-style exhibit.

China More CircleVision 360° scenic highlights, museum-quality displays of historic artefacts from Imperial China and fabulously elaborate architecture.

France Recreated Belle Epoque Paris in the shadow of a miniature Eiffel Tower. Café dining, wine-tasting, waterfront artists and a French perfumerie.

Germany Storybook architecture with geranium-filled window boxes, plus traditional 'oompah' music piped out over the popular *biergarten*.

Italy Venice's St Mark's Square and the Doge's Palace recreated with immaculate scaled-down precision, including ice-creams, arias and a notable restaurant.

Japan Wind chimes, temple drums and a pagoda, set beside manicured gardens and koi fish ponds, give an authentic twist to this shopping and dining complex.

Mexico A huge model of a pre-Columbian pyramid and a boat ride down the River of Time attract plenty of visitors to the colourful Mexican village.

Morocco An attractive Moorish souk set in narrow alleys and elegant tiled courtyards. Authentic belly-dancing displays in the restaurant.

Norway Malevolent trolls summon up a North Sea storm to rock the good ship *Maelstrom* (FP), a Viking longboat thrill ride in this popular Scandinavian village.

United Kingdom – or, rather, Merrie England: a jolly knees-up with Cockney pearly kings and queens in the Rose & Crown Pub, fish and chips, warm beer and street entertainers massacring Shakespeare.

Shop the World
The World Showcase villages offer unusual shopping opportunities. In Morocco's souk, genuine North African leatherwear, carpets, brass items and fezes make interesting souvenirs. Canada offers Indian and Eskimo arts and crafts; there are fine wines and porcelain on sale in the French village; Oriental goodies in China and Japan; and classic cashmere knitwear and Scottish tartans from the United Kingdom.

Epcot Entertainment
Throughout the day, shows, parades and cultural events take place around the park. Check current park guides for details of Mariachi concerts in Mexico, acrobats in Morocco, operetta in Italy and Caledonian bagpipe serenades in Canada. After dark, the 40-acre World Showcase Lagoon is the scene of the dramatic IllumiNations Reflections of Earth firework, laser light and sound spectacular, visible for miles around.

72A3
World Drive, Walt Disney
World Resort
(407) 824 4321
Check current schedules

**Transport to the Magic
Kingdom**
Shuttle buses pick up and
drop off regularly at
Transportation and Ticket
Center
Ferry crosses Seven Seas
Lagoon into Park; also
monorail from
Transportation and Ticket
Center

MAGIC KINGDOM

The Disney theme park that nobody wants to miss is, as a
result, the most crowded, overwhelming and deserving of
a second visit if you have time. Dominated by the
fulsomely turreted and spired fairytale folly of Cinderella
Castle, seven themed lands spread out over the 100-acre
site, and there are 40-plus adventure attractions, dozens of
daily shows, and Disney characters at every turn.

Adventureland Lush tropical plants and eclectic colonial
architecture set the scene for some of the best rides and
adventures in the park. Explore the ingenious Swiss Family
Treehouse, laid out amid the branches of a giant (plastic)
banyan tree, and grab a pith helmet from the explorers'
outfitters for a gentle rainforest Jungle Cruise (FP). The
excellent Pirates of the Caribbean adventure is a rollicking
boat journey into pirate territory with noisy special effects,
Audio-Animatronics buccaneers, caves full of plundered loot
and a marine attack on a Caribbean island. On a less
bloodthirsty note, kids will love dodging the waterspewing
camels on The Magic Carpets of Aladdin,
and singing totem poles and flowers join
feathered Audio-Animatronic friends in
saccharine sweet renditions of songs
from South Seas musicals in The
Enchanted Tiki Room (FP) Under New
Management.

Fantasyland Gathered at the foot of
Cinderella Castle, rides and shows are
based on storybook characters designed
to appeal to smaller children. Classic
fairground rides include the prancing,
gilded horses of Cinderella's Golden
Carrousel, the whirlygig cups and saucers
of the Mad Tea Party and the two-man
pachyderms of Dumbo the Flying
Elephant. Children can enjoy The Many
Adventures of Winnie the Pooh (FP); cool
off playing in the waterspouts at Ariel's
Grotto; or float through the excruciatingly
cute It's a Small World singing doll exhibit.

Frontierland A step back in time to the
Old West with stores, a shooting gallery
and a brace of good thrill rides. The
runaway log flume action at Splash
Mountain (FP) kicks up enough of a wave
to cool off onlookers, while the Big
Thunder Mountain Railroad (FP) takes

Photograph: © Disney

passengers on a whoopin' and hollerin' roller-coaster ride. Motorised rafts potter across to Tom Sawyer Island, a wooded domain which offers a Mystery Mine Shaft, lurching rope-and-barrel bridges, and short trails to Fort Langhorn stockade.

Liberty Square A genteel counterpoint to the bedlam of the neighbouring Frontierland, Liberty Square has a more East Coast colonial feel and a patriotic spreading live oak, known as the Liberty Tree. Here, the worthy Hall of Presidents presentation tackles American history in a series of lectures delivered by Audio-Animatronics US presidents. More lively by far are the undead in the Haunted Mansion (FP). This schlock-horror attraction through curtains of cobwebs, rattling bones and shrieking holograms is more rib-tickling than scary, but it's well worth braving the queues for, nevertheless. In addition, there are boat trips on the Liberty Belle Riverboat; and good times galore to be had at The Diamond Horseshoe Saloon Revue, which seems to have taken root here by mistake just short of Frontierland.

Shows and Parades
Tribute shows in the Castle Forecourt and Fantasyland several times a day. Daily, all-singing, all-dancing parade on Main Street, U.S.A. at 3PM. Check schedules for the SpectroMagic nighttime parade and Fantasy in the Sky Fireworks (daily).

Enjoying a trip on the Liberty Belle Riverboat

Transport within the Magic Kingdom

- Walt Disney World Railroad circles the perimeter of the park, starting at main entrance, with stops at Frontierland and Mickey's Toontown Fair.
  Tomorrowland Transit Authority loop ride operates within Tomorrowland

Cartoon Characters

- Disney Character Greeting Locations, highlighted on free map guides
- Character dining at The Crystal Palace (Main Street); Liberty Tree Tavern (dinner only, Liberty Square); character breakfasts in Fantasyland at Cinderella's Royal Table (reservations from the City Hall information centre). For schedules and reservations:
  ☎ (407) 939 3463

Main Street, U.S.A. A prettified Victorian street scene, said to have been inspired by Walt Disney's childhood home in Marceline, Missouri, this broad avenue leads from the front gate up to Cinderella Castle at the hub of the park. Near the gates, in Town Square, City Hall is the main information centre and depot for the horse-drawn carriages and trams which trundle up Main Street to the castle. The square also has tree-shaded areas where regular concerts are held by the Main Street Rythm Rascals. All along the route to the castle, shops sell a variety of Disney merchandise and gifts. If just arriving at the park has whetted your appetite, there's an ice-cream parlour and a bake shop.

Mickey's Toontown Fair Home to Mickey and Minnie, this colourful corner of the park is a huge favourite with little children. Take a tour around Minnie's Country House – a veritable symphony in lilac and pink hearts and flowers with a garden to match. Mickey's Country House, next door, as you might expect, displays wardrobes full of the signature red trousers, black jackets and big boots and Pluto's dog kennel is in the garden. Children can cool off in the Donald's Boat play area, thoughtfully equipped with a bungee-soft floor and water jets; and there are pint-sized thrills to be had on The Barnstormer at Goofy's Wiseacre Farm roller-coaster.

Tomorrowland Dramatically updated and revamped, there is now lots to see and do here. Top of the list is Space Mountain (FP), an old favourite and terrific roller-coaster ride in the dark that many rate as the top ride in the park. Tomorrowland Indy Speedway is enduringly popular, too. The scarifying ExtraTERRORestrial Alien Encounter subjects the audience (trapped aboard an alien space transporter) to plenty that goes bump in the pitch dark; and there are interactive thrills and spills aboard Buzz Lightyear's Space Ranger Spin (FP) as riders battle the evil Zurg with lasers.

On a rather gentler note, do not miss The Timekeeper, an amusing CircleVision 360° time-travel romp hosted by a duo of smart-talking robots. Take flight in the Astro Orbiter, a mini-rocket ship ride that resembles a chunk of 1950s space cartoon hardware, but does afford a good view of the area, as does the Tomorrowland Transit Authority, which detours into the bowels of Space Mountain to listen to the roller-coaster passengers' screams. Debuted way back at the 1964 New York World's Fair, Walt Disney's Carousel of Progress has its share of loyal fans, but in truth this stilted Audio-Animatronics nostalgia-fest is unlikely to appeal to anybody under 60.

Opposite: Adventureland includes the ride The Magic Carpets of Aladdin

Other Walt Disney World Resort Attractions

BLIZZARD BEACH   ✪✪

Watersports are the speciality of Blizzard Beach, a northern ski-resort-gone-tropical water park, where the chair lifts sport sun umbrellas and the slalom course is a waterslide.

The 60-acre site boasts a dozen different adventure zones in the shadow of 'snow-covered' Mount Gushmore. Take a chair lift up to the 60mph Summit Plummet slide, or the slightly less dramatic Slush Gusher. Other top attractions include the Teamboat Springs white-water raft ride, inner tubing down Runoff Rapids, and the Snow Stormers flumes.

On a less frenetic note, lazy Cross Country Creek circles the park and a sandy beach borders the wave pool below Mt Gushmore. Little children can play safely at Tike's Peak; and there is shopping for essentials and souvenirs in The Village, at the east end of the beach.

DISNEY'S FORT WILDERNESS   ✪✪

Disney's Fort Wilderness offers an enormous range of outdoor activities, from watersports to horse-riding. There are fishing trips for largemouth bass and a children's excursion for bluegill (ages 6–12). Joggers can pound around the 2½ mile jogging trail. Canoes and bicycles are available for rental; sign up for a game of volleyball or basketball; or just work on a tan down at the lakeside beach. Young children also enjoy the petting zoo.

DOWNTOWN DISNEY   ✪✪✪

On the shores of Lake Buena Vista, the ever-expanding Downtown Disney shopping, dining and entertainment complex encompasses three distinct districts: the Marketplace; Pleasure Island (➤ below); and the rapidly expanding West Side attractions area.

Down on the lakeside, the Marketplace combines a selection of colourful boutiques and souvenir shopping outlets (➤ 104, 106) with a handful of restaurants, including the landmark Rainforest Café (➤ 99), crowned by a smoking volcano. During the day there are pedalboats for hire from the dock.

The neon-lit West Side boasts the state-of-the-art DisneyQuest interactive games attraction, a 24-screen cinema complex, Virgin Records Megastore, and the Cirque du Soleil, a 1,650-seat theatre which stages glitzy, high-energy acrobatic and modern dance productions. Notable dining and entertainment venues include

Orlando outposts of the House of Blues, Planet Hollywood, Wolfgang Puck Café and Gloria Estefan's Bongos Cuban Café.

PLEASURE ISLAND ✪✪✪

A six-acre nighttime entertainment complex, Pleasure Island's one-off admission ticket entitles guests to party the night away in any or all of its eight night clubs. There is also shopping, dining, movie theatres and dancing in the streets. Several of the shops are open during the day, when admission is free, but the real action (and paid admission) starts at 7PM and builds to a midnight New Year's Eve Street Party, complete with fireworks and a

🔟 72B2

✉ E Buena Vista Drive, Walt Disney World Resort

☎ (407) 939 2648

🕐 Daily, shops 10AM–1AM; clubs 7PM–2AM

🍴 Light dining in the clubs (££), also access to the Marketplace restaurants (➤ 97–9)

♿ Good

💰 Expensive (or available as option with Park Hopper Plus Pass). Additional charge for movie theatres. Occasional additional charge for special shows in specific clubs

🔁 Downtown Disney (➤ above)

❓ Under 18s must be accompanied by a parent; for admission to BET Soundstage Club and Mannequins guests must be 21 or older. All guests need passport, driving licence or birth certificate to buy alcohol

Pleasure Island has the nightlife scene covered

89

Shark Reef at Disney's Typhoon Lagoon water park

blizzard of confetti every night of the year. The revelry continues until 2AM.

The night clubs run the gamut from The Comedy Warehouse, with its nightly improvisational comedy shows, to the Rock N Roll Beach Club, which serves up live bands and DJs spinning hits from the 1960s up to the present day. Need to unwind after a hectic day? The check out the laidback sounds in the Pleasure Island Jazz Company. Still got energy to burn? Lava lamps and mirror balls are all the rage at 1970s-style 8TRAX; for more contemporary sounds, hit Motion, Mannequins Dance Palace or the BET Soundstage™ Club for the best in high-energy hip-hop and R&B. For something completely different, sample the interactive comedy and general weirdness on offer at the Adventurers Club.

TYPHOON LAGOON ✪✪✪

A truly impressive water park complex with an artfully shipwrecked air, Typhoon Lagoon's showpiece is the 2½-acre lagoon with surf-sized 6-foot waves rolling onto sandy beaches every 90 seconds. Rocky Mount Mayday is landscaped with flumes and waterslides, and snorkellers can explore the 362,000-gallon salt-water coral reef environment, Shark Reef, inhabited by real tropical fish. For the biggest thrills in the park, though, check out Humunga Kowabunga, an awesome trio of 30mph waterslides. The Keelhowl Falls Whitewater rafting adventure is also highly recommended; and there is the separate Ketchakidee Creek water playground for little children.

➕ 72B1

✉ Epcot Center Drive, Walt Disney World Resort

☎ (407) 824 4321

🕐 Daily 10–5 (extended summer and hols)

🍴 Leaning Palms (£), Typhoon Tilly's (£)

♿ Few

💲 Expensive (or available as option with Park Hopper Plus Pass)

Where To...

Above: *King Henry's Banquet, International Drive*
Right: *a kung fu demonstration in Splendid China*

Orlando

Prices

Prices are approximate, based on a three-course meal for one without drinks and service:

£ = under $15
££ = $15 to $30
£££ = over $30

B-Line Diner (££)
Fun 1950s-style diner in the smart Peabody Orlando hotel (Dux ➤ 93, and Peabody Orlando ➤ 101). Sandwiches, salads, pizzas and milkshakes are served; service is available 24 hours a day, and there is a take-out counter.

✉ Peabody Orlando, 9801 International Drive ☎ (407) 345 4460 🕐 Breakfast, lunch and dinner 🚌 I-Ride, Lynx #42

Bergamo's (££)
This jolly Italian restaurant serves home-made pasta, fresh seafood dishes and steaks and other hearty dishes to the accompaniment of its famous singing waiters.

✉ The Mercado, 8445 International Drive ☎ (407) 352 3805 🕐 Dinner only 🚌 I-Ride, Lynx #42

Café Tu Tu Tango (£)
A jumbled artist's loft-themed dining room with genuine painters daubing away on site. You can order from a wide choice of multi-ethnic appetizer-size eats (tapas-style) and sample the sangria.

✉ 8625 International Drive ☎ (407) 248 2222 🕐 Lunch and dinner 🚌 I-Ride, Lynx #42

California Pizza Kitchen(£)
Planning a trip to the mall? This innovative pizza chain makes a great re-fuelling stop when the shopping gets too much. Also pastas, salads sups and puds.

✉ The Florida Mall, 8001 S Orange Blossom Trail ☎ (407) 854 5741 Lunch and dinner and ✉ Mall at Millenia, 4200 Conroy Road ☎ (407) 370 2542 Lunch and dinner

Charley's Steak House (££)
Voted one of the Top Ten Steak Houses in the US by The Knife & Fork Club of America, Charley's serves prime aged beef cooked over a wood fire in a specially built pit. There's good seafood, too.

✉ Goodings Plaza, 8255 International Drive ☎ (407) 363 0228 🕐 Dinner only 🚌 I-Ride, Lynx #42

Charlie's Lobster House (££)
Fresh Maine lobster served eight different ways, a long menu of straight seafood and tasty variations such as the house speciality Maryland crab cakes. There is a good wine list and live jazz is performed.

✉ The Mercado, 8445 International Drive ☎ (407) 352 6929 🕐 Dinner only 🚌 I-Ride, Lynx #42

Christini's Ristorante Italiano (£££)
Gourmet AAA Four-Diamond Italian restaurant. Classical cuisine with some light modern touches; one of the chef's star turns is *fettucini alla Christini*. Smart dress; charming service.

✉ The Marketplace, 7600 Dr Phillips Boulevard/Sand Lake Road ☎ (407) 345 8770 🕐 Dinner only

Coq au Vin (££–£££)
This one is something of a rarity: a Central Florida French restaurant which has a long-standing reputation for producing well-prepared classics in a relaxing atmosphere.

✉ 4800 S Orange Avenue ☎ (407) 851 6980 🕐 Tue–Sun lunch and dinner

Damon's The Place for Ribs (££)

An old favourite for no-nonsense barbecued fare. Mouth-watering, juicy ribs are served up with the house special sauce and prime aged beef.

✉ The Mercado/Suite 108, 8445 International Drive ☎ (407) 352 5984 🕐 Mon–Fri lunch only, Sat–Sun open 3PM–10PM 🚌 I-Ride, Lynx #42

Dux (£££)

The Peabody Orlando's award-winning signature restaurant. Elegant décor, sophisticated New American cuisine and an excellent wine cellar are all part of the package. (Jackets for men.) The hotel also boasts a fine northern Italian restaurant, Capriccio, in a less formal setting.

✉ Peabody Orlando, 9801 International Drive ☎ (407) 345 4550 🕐 Mon–Sat, dinner only 🚌 I-Ride, Lynx #42

Flippers Pizza (£)

Well-priced local pizza chain specialising in hand-tossed, made-to-order pizzas, baked pasta dishes, salads and dips.

✉ 4774 Kirkman Road ☎ (407) 521 0607 and ✉ 7480 Universal Boulevard ☎ (407) 351 5643 🕐 Lunch and dinner

Hard Rock Café (££)

An Orlando outpost for the world's largest Hard Rock Café. The self-styled 'Coliseum of Rock' at Universal Studios sits next to the Hard Rock Live auditorium and the dining area contains the usual impressive display of rock memorabilia including Elvis's Gibson guitar, the Beatles' 1960s suits and a surfboard autographed by Jan and Dean. On the menu you'll find all-American burgers, hickory-smoked barbecue chicken, salads and the charmingly named house speciality, Pig Sandwich.

✉ Universal's CityWalk ☎ (407) 351 7625 🕐 Lunch and dinner

Jimmy Buffett's Margaritaville (££)

A casual Key West-style eatery and bar serving up mega cheeseburgers, name-sake margaritas and a side order of Jimmy Buffett tunes.

✉ Universal's CityWalk ☎ (407) 224 6916 🕐 Lunch and dinner

Lombard's Landing (££–£££)

San Francisco-style seafood restaurant, all red brick and curly ironwork, overlooking the lagoon at the heart of Universal Studios. There is a big deck for outdoor dining, fresh seafood specials, pasta and burgers. Dinner reservations advisable in season.

✉ Universal Studios, 1000 Universal Studios Plaza ☎ (407) 224 6401 🕐 Lunch and dinner

McDonalds (£)

The world's largest McDonalds on the corner of International Drive. Whacky architecture incorporates built-in french fries. You'll find the usual burgers, plus pizzas and a video games room.

✉ 6875 Sand Lake Road ☎ (407) 351 2185 🕐 24 hours 🚌 I-Ride, Lynx #42

Dux Delight

Ever since a couple of well-refreshed hunters jokingly popped their live decoy ducks in the fountain of the Peabody Memphis over a century ago, the Peabody people have had a thing for ducks. Twice daily (11AM and 5PM) The Peabody Orlando's marching mallards parade through the main lobby between their daily duties of circling the fountain and their $100,000 Royal Duck Palace. Take afternoon tea – and a camera! (► 101)

The Real Lili Marlene

German lyricist Hans Leip was on sentry duty during World War I when he began to write a song inspired by his girlfriend Lili, and his best friend's girl, Marleen. Finally set to music in 1938, *Lili Marlene* was already a hit in Germany when the Allies heard it on Nazi propaganda radio in North Africa in 1941, and adopted it as their own. Later US forces' sweetheart Marlene Dietrich made a celebrated version.

McCormick R Schmick's (££)

Traditional seafood house tucked into a modern mall. The fresh seafood is flown in from the Atlantic and Pacific coasts daily and varies with the season.

✉ Mall at Millenia, 4200 Conroy Road ☎ (407) 226 6515 🕐 Lunch and dinner

Manuel's on the 28th (£££)

Downtown's most exclusive dining room with spectacular views from the 28th floor of the NationsBank Center. Sophisticated continental-'Floribbean' cuisine. Jackets preferred.

✉ 390 N Orange Avenue ☎ (407) 246 6580 🕐 Dinner only

Ming Court (£££)

Stylish Chinese restaurant with views over manicured Oriental gardens, mini waterfalls and koi ponds. Very good fresh seafood, and there are steaks and grills as well as skilfully prepared Chinese cuisine; *dim sum* trolley at lunchtime.

✉ 9188 International Drive ☎ (407) 351 9988 🕐 Lunch and dinner 🚌 I-Ride, Lynx #42

Numero Uno (£)

Small and friendly Latin American restaurant with generous portion control and a hearty menu of filling staples from paella Valencia to roast pork and black beans, steaks and seafood.

✉ 2499 S Orange Avenue ☎ (407) 841 3840 🕐 Lunch Mon–Fri, dinner Mon–Sat

Olive Garden (£–££)

Popular chain of cheap and cheerful Italian restaurants at several locations around Orlando.

✉ 8984 International Drive ☎ (407) 264 0420 🕐 Lunch and dinner 🚌 I-Ride, Lynx #42

Race Rock (££)

Motor racing memorabilia and rock music in a heaven-sent dining opportunity for boy racers (➤ 95, panel). First-class pizzas, pasta, burgers and fiery chicken wings.

✉ 8986 International Drive ☎ (407) 248 9876 🕐 Lunch and dinner 🚌 I-Ride, Lunx #42

Ran-Getsu (£££)

Authenic Japanese cuisine and an attractive location overlooking a Japanese garden and koi pond. Chefs prepare traditional *sushi*, *sukiyaki* and *tempura*. Entertainment at weekends.

✉ 8400 International Drive ☎ (407) 345 0044 🕐 Dinner. only 🚌 I-Ride, Lynx #42

Roy's Orlando (££–£££)

One of Orlando's gourmet hot spots. Chef Greg Richie blends western techniques with Asian ingredients and a dash of Hawaiian inspiration to create fabulous fusion cuisine. Unusual but well balanced combinations such as the mouth-watering seared scallops with wasabi sweet ginger butter.

✉ 7760 W Sand Lake Road ☎ (407) 352 4844 🕐 Dinner only 🚌 I-Ride, Lynx #42

Samba Room

A Latin café with rhythm and South American–Caribbean panache. Cocktails and spiced rums, seafood, grilled meats, exotic fruits and the Bossa Nova.

7468 W Sand Lake Road (407) 226 0550 or I-800 713 9106 Lunch and dinner I-Ride, Lynx #42

Around Orlando

Altamonte Springs

Gina's on the Water (££)
Cosy little Italian restaurant across the street from Crane's Roost Lane. Excellent seafood speciality and pasta dishes. Outdoor seating; entertainment Fri–Sat evenings.
✉ 309 N North Lake Boulevard ☎ (407) 834 5880 🕐 Lunch and dinner

Kissimmee

Giordano's of Kissimmee (£–££)
Always busy with visitors and locals, this family-friendly Chicago-style pizzeria also servies a selection of other favourite Italian dishes.
✉ 7866 W Irlo Bronson Memorial Highway/US192 ☎ (407) 397 0044 and ✉ 12151 S Apopka-Vineland Road, Lake Buena Vista ☎ (407) 239 8900 🕐 Lunch and dinner

JT's Prime Time (£–££)
The all-you-can-eat Prime Rib Special is the mainstay at this budget family restaurant west of I-4. Also steaks and chicken, children's menu and games room.
✉ 8553 W Irlo Bronson Memorial Highway/US192 ☎ (407) 239 6555 🕐 Lunch and dinner

Key W Kool's Oak Grill (££)
Nautical décor with a nod towards the Florida Keys and a steak and seafood grill menu fresh from the oakwood pit barbecue.
✉ 7725 W US192 (west of I-4) ☎ (407) 239 7166 🕐 Dinner

Pacino's (££)
Family-owned modern trattoria serving home-made bread and operettas, good pasta dishes, seafood, and other Italian favourites.
✉ 5795 W US192 ☎ (407) 396 6288 🕐 Dinner only

Ponderosa Steakhouse (£)
All-you-can-eat family restaurant chain featuring a groaning buffet table. Pay for an entrée then load up with soup, salad, pasta, chilli, shrimp, desserts, and more.
✉ 7598 W Irlo Bronson Memorial Highway/US192 ☎ (407) 396 7721 🕐 Breakfast, lunch and dinner

Punjab Indian Restaurant (£–££)
Spicing up the dining options on US192, the Punjab serves tasty mild, medium and hot curries, as well as all the usual tempting Indian side dishes.
✉ 3404 W Vine Street/US192 ☎ (407) 931 2449 🕐 Tue–Sat lunch and dinner, Sun–Mon dinner only

Red Lobster (££)
Popular seafood restaurant chain offering a wide choice of fresh fish dishes as well as seafood pasta, steak and chicken. Families are welcome; there is a special children's menu.
✉ 4010 W Vine Street/US192 ☎ (407) 846 3513 🕐 Lunch and dinner

Rovers Return (£–££)
Homesick Brits in search of pub grub and a warm welcome should make tracks for this home-style pub serving steak and kidney pud and other old favourites as well as British beers. Children welcome.
✉ 3620 W Vine Street ☎ (407) 870 1535 🕐 Lunch and dinner

Race Rock
Dine in the fast lane at this landmark racing-themed restaurant with a distinctive chequered flag roof (▶ 94). Celebrity partners include Richard and Kyle Petty, Michael Andretti and Don Prudhomme. The foyer is a monument to high-octane horsepower decked out with Formula One and Indy cars, dragsters, motorcycles, and speedboats. Video screens show racing footage, there are video games and, of course, a chance to stock up on Race Rock merchandise.

95

Picnics for the Park

Goodings, a well-stocked local supermarket chain, is the place to stock up for a picnic at one of the Central Florida state parks. There are branches at Goodings International Plaza (next to The Mercado), 8255 International Drive; and Crossroads of Lake Buena Vista, 12541 SR535 (opposite Hotel Plaza Boulevard). Concessions in the parks sell snacks and there are vending machines for cold drinks.

SummerHouse-Hyatt (££)
Breakfast buffet followed by a day-long menu of tasty sandwiches, Mexican dishes, steaks and Cuisine Naturelle healthy options. Children 12 and under half-price.
✉ **Hyatt Orlando, 6375 W Irlo Bronson Memorial Highway/US192** ☎ **(407) 396 1234 ext 5005** 🕐 **Breakfast, lunch and dinner**

Lake Wales
Chalet Suzanne (£££)
Award-winning restaurant in a lovely country inn (➤ 103), Chalet Suzanne's cosy, antique-filled dining room overlooks a small lake. The excellent American-Continental menu is short, the wine list long, the service attentive.
✉ **3800 Chalet Suzanne Drive (off CR17A, 4.5 miles north of Lake Wales)** ☎ **(863) 676 6011 or 1-800 433 6011** 🕐 **Lunch and dinner. Closed Mon**

Longwood
Enzo's on the Lake (££–£££)
Lakefront Italian dining room with a thoroughly Mediterranean feel and atmosphere. Fish soup with crab and *buccatin alla Enzo* (pasta with a robust mushroom-bacon-pea sauce) are the delicious house specialities.
✉ **1130 US17-92** ☎ **(407) 834 9872** 🕐 **Lunch Mon–Fri, dinner Mon–Sat**

Mount Dora
The Beauclaire (££–£££)
Charming formal dining room in an historic lakeside inn. Gourmet dinner menu, but a more casual approach at lunchtime, when there are tables on the veranda and a choice of salads, light chicken and fish dishes. Very popular venue for Sunday brunch.
✉ **Lakeside Inn, 100 N Alexander Street** ☎ **(352) 383 4101** 🕐 **Lunch and dinner**

Windsor Rose English Tea Room (£)
Welcoming tea room with a gift and garden shop attached. Traditional Cornish pasties, Scotch eggs and Ploughman's (bread and cheese) lunches, as well as home-made scones and cakes.
✉ **144 W 4th Avenue** ☎ **(352) 735 2551** 🕐 **Morning coffee, lunch and tea**

Winter Park
Panera Bread (£)
A great lunch stop close to Rollins College. This bakery-cum-café chain is hugely popular and good value. Tuck into homemade soup in a sourdough bread bowl, sandwiches, salads and frothy cappuccinos with a pastry on the side.
✉ **118 W Fairbanks Avenue** ☎ **(407) 645 3939** 🕐 **Breakfast, lunch and dinner**

Park Plaza Gardens (£££)
An elegant New Orleans-style covered courtyard provides the setting for award-winning Florida cuisine. Creative dishes are served, employing the freshest local ingredients, there is a fine wine list and the service is exemplary. Sunday brunch is a local institution.
✉ **319 Park Avenue South** ☎ **(407) 645 2475** 🕐 **Lunch and dinner**

Walt Disney World Resort and Lake Buena Vista

Arthur's 27 (£££)

International cuisine, elegant surroundings and panoramic views over the Walt Disney World Resort nighttime firework displays. A choice of *prix-fixe* menus as well as *à la carte* specialities. Reservations advised.

✉ **Wyndham Palace Resort & Spa, 1900 Buena Vista Drive**
☎ **(407) 827 3450 or 1-800 327 2990** 🍴 **Dinner only**

Artist Point (££–£££)

Hearty cooking from the Pacific Northwest fits right in with the Wilderness Lodge decor. Salmon, Penn Cove mussels, game dishes and a notable wine list.

✉ **Disney's Wilderness Lodge, Magic Kingdom Resort Area**
☎ **(407) 939 3463**
🍴 **Breakfast and dinner**

Benihana of Tokyo Inc at Hilton in the WDW Resort (£££)

Popular Japanese-American restaurant chain serving grilled steaks, seafood and chicken dishes prepared right before your eyes.

✉ **1751 Hotel Plaza Boulevard**
☎ **(407) 827 4865** 🍴 **Dinner only**

Big River Brewing Company at Disney's Boardwalk (££)

Visitors can watch beer being made and then sample the daily brew at Disney's very own on-site micro-brewery. Outdoor seating and a casual dining menu.

✉ **Disney's BoardWalk, 2101 N Epcot Resorts Boulevard**
☎ **(407) 560 0253** 🍴 **Lunch and dinner**

Boma – Flavors of Africa (£)

A 'marketplace' eating experience with wood-burning grills where African-inspired cuisine and flavoursome Indian and African style dishes are prepared from market-fresh fish, meats and vegetables.

✉ **Disney's Animal Kingdom Lodge, Lake Buena Vista**
☎ **(407) 939 3463**
🍴 **Breakfast and dinner**

Bongos Cuban Café (££–£££)

Restaurant and nightclub created by Miami's disco queen, Gloria Estefan, and husband Emilio. Authentic Cuban-Latin American music and food.

✉ **Downtown Disney West Side** ☎ **(407) 828 0999**
🍴 **Breakfast, lunch and dinner**

California Grill (££)

Stylish Californian cuisine with views over Magic Kingdom. Watch the delicious designer pizzas, oak-fired beef tenderloin and seared tuna steaks being prepared in the open-to-view kitchen.

✉ **Disney's Contemporary Resort, Magic Kingdom Resort Area** ☎ **(407) 939 3463**
🍴 **Dinner only**

Chef Mickey's (££)

Disney character dining guaranteed to delight the children. All-you-can-eat breakfasts and a dinner buffet that's served from 5PM to accommodate a sensible bedtime after a day in the park (▶ panel).

✉ **Disney's Contemporary Resort, 4600 N World Drive**
☎ **(407) 939 3463**
🍴 **Breakfast and dinner**

Disney Character Dining

A sure-fire hit with children, there are plenty of opportunities to dine out with favourite cartoon characters. Minnie Mouse hosts breakfast at the 'Ohana in Disney's Polynesian Resort; Winnie the Pooh, Eeyore and Tigger tuck in at The Crystal Palace Buffet in Magic Kingdom; and Admiral Goofy and crew attend the Cape May Café breakfast buffet at the Disney Beach Club Resort. Check schedules and make reservations for these and other sightings (☎ (407) 939 3463). See also ▶ 86.

Rainforest Café

A smoking, 65-foot-high mini-volcano in the middle of Downtown Disney? Unbelievable. But then so is the Rainforest Café, brainchild of Steven Schussler, entrepreneur and eco-warrior, who once moved all the furniture out of his house to improve the environment for his pet parrots. Immersed in the simulated rainforest, marvel at the live and animated wildlife, feel the creeping mist and be assured that all the ingredients are environmentally correct.

Chefs de France (£££)

A triumvirate of top French chefs (Bocuse, Vergé and Lenôtre) provided the creative inspiration behind this up-market restaurant in Epcot's World Showcase. For this reason it is one of the most popular dining options in the park, so reservations are a must.

✉ **Epcot , Epcot Center Drive** ☎ **(407) 939 3463** 🕐 **Lunch and dinner**

Chevy's Mexican Restaurant (££)

Friendly service and good, fast Mexican food in a barn-like dining room. The sizzling mesquite-grilled *fajitas* are especially recommended.

✉ **Crossroads of Lake Buena Vista, 12547 SR535** ☎ **(407) 827 1052** 🕐 **Lunch and dinner**

Fulton's Crab House (£££)

Housed in a replica turn-of-the-last-century riverboat permanently moored to the shore of Lake Buena Vista, this seafood restaurant is popular, so be prepared to have to queue for dinner. It's usually worth it for the enormous choice of expertly prepared fresh fish, a raw bar, and a notable sour cherry cobbler for dessert.

✉ **Downtown Disney Marketplace, 1670 E Buena Vista Drive** ☎ **(407) 934 2628** 🕐 **Lunch and dinner**

The Hollywood Brown Derby (££)

A faithful re-creation of Hollywood's famous Brown Derby restaurant, featuring comfortable 1930s-style décor.

✉ **Disney-MGM Studios, W Buena Vista Drive** ☎ **(407) 939 3463** 🕐 **Lunch and dinner**

L'Originale Alfredo di Roma Ristorante (££–£££)

One of the stars in Epcot's culinary crown and very popular. Sample the namesake *fettucine alfredo*, seafood, veal dishes and Italian wines, all served to the sound of the singing waiters.

✉ **World Showcase, Epcot, Epcot Center Drive** ☎ **(407) 939 3463** 🕐 **Lunch and dinner**

Official All Star Café (£–££)

Glitzy eatery lavishly adorned with all-star sporting memorabilia, wall-to-wall video monitors screening great sporting moments, pumping music and a menu featuring burgers, hot dogs, steaks and ribs.

✉ **Disney's Wide World of Sports, 1701 W Buena Vista Drive** ☎ **(407) 939 5000** 🕐 **Lunch and dinner**

'Ohana (££–£££)

Polynesian-style family feasts served up in atmospheric South Seas surroundings with a barbecue firepit.

✉ **Disney's Polynesian Resort, 1600 Seven Seas Drive** ☎ **(407) 939 3463** 🕐 **Dinner only**

Lake Buena Vista Ale House (£–££)

Casual nautical décor and big-screen TVs for sporting events coverage. Steaks, ribs and seafood, plus 56 beers on tap.

✉ **12371 Winter Garden-Vineland Road** ☎ **(407) 239 1800** 🕐 **Lunch and dinner**

The Outback (££–£££)

Australian-themed restaurant with a three-storey waterfall and flourishing greenery, plus steaks, seafood and a storyteller recounting tales from the bush.

✉ **Wyndham Palace Resort & Spa, 1900 Buena Vista Drive** ☎ **(407) 827 3430** 🕐 **Dinner only**

Pebbles (££–£££)
Creative New American cuisine for the 'casual gourmet'. Delicious salads, seafood and poultry. Relaxed, friendly atmosphere. A local favourite, with a second outpost in downtown's Church Street district. (► 94)
✉ **12551 SR535** ☎ **(407) 827 1111** 🕐 **Lunch and dinner**

Planet Hollywood (££)
Film and television memorabilia in all shapes and sizes from the runaway bus in *Speed* to venerable collectables such as Gene Kelly's costume from *Singing in the Rain*. Brash, noisy, packed and planet-shaped; a convenient aperitif for a night out at Pleasure Island.
✉ **Downtown Disney West Side, 1506 E Buena Vista Drive** ☎ **(407) 827 7836** 🕐 **Lunch and dinner**

Portobello Yacht Club (££–£££)
Generous Northern Italian cooking, featuring mountains of home-made pasta, pizzas cooked in a wood-burning brick oven and daily specials with the emphasis on fresh seafood. Bustling casual atmosphere and waterfront terrace dining overlooking Lake Buena Vista.
✉ **Downtown Disney (just outside Pleasure Island), 1650 E Buena Vista Drive** ☎ **(407) 934 8888** 🕐 **Lunch and dinner**

Rainforest Café (££–£££)
Enormously popular jungle-themed restaurant swathed in deepest tropical décor. Trees and waterfalls, parrots and piña coladas. Broad menu of American favourites with a Caribbean twist (► 98, panel). Also at Animal Kingdom.
✉ **Downtown Disney Marketplace, 1800 E Buena Vista Drive** ☎ **(407) 933 2800** 🕐 **Lunch and dinner**

Sassagoula Floatworks and Food Factory (£)
Mardi Gras parade props decorate this Disney budget dining option. American and Creole menu from burgers and pizza to fried chicken and sweet, deep-fried *beignets* (doughnuts).
✉ **Disney's Port Orleans Resort, 2201 Orleans Drive** ☎ **(407) 939 3463** 🕐 **Breakfast, lunch and dinner**

Spoodles (££–£££)
Fresh and appetizing Mediterranean menu from wood-fired thin-crust pizzas to Greek *mezes*, North African houmous, kebabs and salads. Steak and seafood also on offer.
✉ **Disney's BroadWalk, Epcot Resort Area** ☎ **(407) 939 3463** 🕐 **Breakfast and dinner**

Wolfgang Puck Grand Café (££–£££)
Celebrity chef Wolfgang Puck popularised the designer pizza. Wood-fired pizzas feature smoked salmon, spicy chicken, Chinese duck and esoteric Italian cheeses. Also has a stall in the Marketplace.
✉ **Downtown Disney (West Side)** ☎ **(407) 938 9653** 🕐 **Lunch and dinner**

Dining with Children
Not surprisingly, most Orlando restaurants welcome children. Family restaurants, burger chains and a wide choice of budget dining options abound around the International Drive resort area and Kissimmee. Many smarter restaurants are equally child-friendly and discounted children's menus are widely available; if you don't see one on display always ask.

Orlando

Prices

The following price bands are given on a per night minimum for a standard room regardless of single, double or multi-person occupancy:

£   = under $60
££   = $60 to 120
£££ = over $120

It is worth noting that many Orlando hotels make no additional charge for children aged 17 or under sharing with their parents.

Ameri Suites (££)

Well-priced suite hotel close to Universal orlando. Living-dining area and separate bedroom, wtih kitchen, pool, exercise room and breakfast buttfet, plus bus to attractions.

✉ **5895 Caravan Court**
☎ **(407) 351 0627 or 1-800 833 1516**

Arnold Palmer's Bay Hill Club & Lodge (££–£££)

A good option for golfers who would like to combine sightseeing with a challenging swing around Arnold Palmer's home course. Sixty-one rooms; dining; pool and tennis.

✉ **9000 Bay Hill Boulevard (west of I-4/Exit 29)** ☎ **(407) 876 2429**

Best Western Plaza International (£–££)

Well-equipped chain hotel midway down International Drive; 672 rooms and suites; pool; dining; airport bus.

✉ **8738 International Drive**
☎ **(407) 345 8195 or 1-800 654 7160** 🚌 **I-Ride, Lynx #42**

Rosen Plaza Hotel (£££)

Elegant executive-type hotel close to the Convention Center; 800 rooms; pool; restaurants.

✉ **9700 International Drive**
☎ **(407) 996 9700 or 1-800 366 9700** 🚌 **I-Ride, Lynx #42**

Days Inn International Drive (£–££)

Central chain hotel just north of Sand Lake Road with 240 budget rooms; pool; restaurant.

✉ **7200 International Drive**
☎ **(407) 351 1200 or 1-800 224 5057** 🚌 **I-Ride, Lynx #42**

Orlando Embassy Suites International Drive South (£££)

Well-priced two-room suites sleeping up to six people in a central location. Pools; fitness centre; Family Fun Center; complimentary cooked breakfast.

✉ **8978 International Drive**
☎ **(407) 352 1400 or 1-800 433 7275** 🚌 **I-Ride, Lynx #42**

Fairfield Inn by Marriott (£–££)

Quiet corner close to I-Drive and dining options. 135 spotless, comfortable rooms; pool, complimentary continental breakfast.

✉ **8342 Jamaican Court**
☎ **(407) 363 1944 or 1-800 228 2800**

Hampton Inn – International Drive Area (££)

Set back just east of I-Drive. 336 rooms, all with fridge and microwave; pool; complimentary breakfast. Also a second Orlando location, just south of Universal Orlando.

✉ **6101 Sand Lake Road**
☎ **(407) 763 7886 or 1-800 763 1100** ✉ **7110 S Kirkman Road**
☎ **(407) 345 1112 or 1-800 763 1100**

Holiday Inn International Drive Resort (££)

Reliable budget- to mid-range chain with more than a dozen Orlando/Kissimmee locations; this one, near Wet 'n Wild, has 652 rooms and suites; pools; restaurants; good children's facilities and baby-sitting services by arrangement.

✉ **6515 International Drive**
☎ **(407) 351 3500 or 1-800 206 2747** 🚌 **I-Ride, Lynx #42**

Hyatt Regency Orlando International Airport (££–£££)

Attractive airport hotel with direct access from the terminal; 446 spacious and functional rooms and suites; restaurants and bar; pool.

✉ **9300 Airport Boulevard**
☎ **(407) 825 1234 or 1-800 233 1234** 🚌 **Lynx #42**

Orlando World Center Marriott (£££)

A huge and very slick resort hotel with 2,000 rooms. Choice of restaurants from fine dining to pizza; pools, 18-hole golf course, lighted tennis courts and health club; good children's facilities, including baby-sitting services.

✉ **8701 World Center Drive**
☎ **(407) 239 4200 or 1-800 621 0638** 🚌 **I-Ride, Lynx #42**

The Peabody Orlando (£££)

High-rise luxury (AAA Four-Diamond) opposite the Convention Center, with 949 attractive and spacious rooms and suites with a view; pool, tennis, health club; golf by arrangement. Restaurants including gourmet dining at Dux (▶ 93).

✉ **9801 International Drive**
☎ **(407) 345 4522 or 1-800 423 8257** 🚌 **I-Ride, Lynx #42**

Portofino Bay at Universal Orlando (£££)

Luxurious Italian Riviera-themed complex with boat transport to the theme parks. There are 750 lovely rooms; a dining area, waterfront boats, swimming pools and childminding facilities.

✉ **5601 Universal Boulevard**
☎ **(407) 224 7117 or 1-877 837 2273**

Radisson at the Entrance to Universal Orlando (££)

Very reasonably priced rooms and suites (742) near Universal. Excellent amenities include dining and a late night lounge; pool; shopping arcade; children's playground.

✉ **5780 Major Boulevard**
☎ **(407) 351 1000 or 1-800 327 2110**

Ramada Inn All Suites by International Drive Center (£££)

Well designed two-bed, two-bath suites (160) with fully equipped kitchens set in a resort complex. Golf course; fishing lake; paddleboats; volleyball; swimming pool; restaurants; children's playground; exercise centre.

✉ **6800 Villa DeCosta Drive**
☎ **(407) 239 0707 or 1-800 633 1405**

Howard Johnson Suites (££)

Suite hotel near Universal; 96 two-room efficiencies with kitchen and patio. Swimming pool, spa, fitness centre and tennis, plus picnic areas with barbecue grills.

✉ **4601 S Kirkman Road** ☎ **(407) 313 1000 or 1-800 826 8515**

Summerfield Suites by Wyndham – International Drive (£££)

Convenient for all the sights, as well as for the shopping and dining on I-Drive: 146 one- to three-bed units which can sleep up to eight people. Swimming pool; bar. Also at Lake Buena Vista.

✉ **8480 International Drive**
☎ **(407) 352 2400 or 1-800 833 4353** 🚌 **I-Ride, Lynx #42**
✉ **8751 Suiteside Drive, Lake Buena Vista** ☎ **(407) 238 0777**

Bookings

Reservations can be made by phone, fax or mail, and should be made as early as possible. A deposit (usually by credit card) equivalent to the nightly rate will ensure that your room is held until 6PM; if you are arriving later, inform the hotel. Credit card is the preferred payment method; travellers' cheques and cash are also acceptable, but payment may have to be made in advance. The final bill will include Florida's 6 per cent sales tax and local resort taxes.

Rooms, Suites and Efficiencies

Rooms in American hotels are generally large, with two double beds as standard. Suites, with two or three separate rooms, are increasingly common and are a good option for families. Efficiencies are rooms with a kitchenette, as well as a separate bathroom.

Around Orlando

Spa Treatment
Footsore and weary after a day at Disney? The Wyndham Palace's superb spa has the answer with its special Theme Park Foot Relief Massage. Spa guests (non-hotel residents welcome) can choose from a tempting array of more than 30 face and body treatments, ranging from aromatherapy to mineral baths. Book in for a single treatment or a half-day, full-day or weekend of luxurious pampering. Additional facilities include a Fitness Center, saunas, and beauty salon.

Kissimmee

Best Western Suite Resort on Lake Cecile (££)
Very reasonable all-suite resort with 158 units. Fully equipped kitchens (including dishwasher); pool and tennis; bar; laundry.
✉ **4786 W Irlo Bronson Memorial Highway/US192**
☎ **(407) 396 2056 or 1-800 468 3687**

Clarion Hotel Maingate (££)
The 198 rooms on two storeys; pool and jacuzzi; fitness centre; dining; other restaurants and shopping within walking distance.
✉ **7675 W Irlo Bronson Memorial Highway/US192**
☎ **(407) 396 4000 or 1-800 568 3352**

Days Inn Maingate East (£–££)
An old-time pastel-painted façade conceals a well-equipped budget bet. 404 rooms, pool, dining WDW and airport shuttles.
✉ **5840 W 1110 Bronson Memorial Highway/US192**
☎ **(407) 396 7069 or 1-800 327 9126**

Econolodge Maingate Resort (£–££)
A budget option earning consistently good reports. Pool and restaurant, shuttle service, car rental.
✉ **7514 W Irlo Bronson Memorial Highway/US192**
☎ **(407) 396 2000 or 1-800 365 6935**

HoJo Maingate East (££)
Reasonably spacious rooms (567), including 197 efficiencies with fully equipped kitchens. Two pools and a playground; close to dining and shopping.
✉ **6051 W Irlo Bronson Memorial Highway/US192**
☎ **(407) 396 1748 or 1-800 288 4678**

Homewood Suites by Hilton (£££)
AAA Three-Diamond 156-suite hotel. Pool and spa; complimentary continental breakfast; pets allowed.
✉ **3100 Parkway Boulevard**
☎ **(407) 396 2229 or 1-888 351 9100**

Hostelling International – Orlando/Kissimmee Resort (£)
Central location with lake frontage and 166 beds in rooms and dormitories. Pool, laundry, Disney shuttles and bargain rates.
✉ **4840 W Irlo Bronson Memorial Highway/US192**
☎ **(407) 396 8282 or 1-800 909 4776 ext 33**

Larson Inn Family Suites (£–££)
166 family rooms and efficiency suites next to Water Mania. Pool, jacuzzi, laundry. Free coffee and papers.
✉ **6075 W Irlo Bronson Memorial Highway/US192** ☎ **(407) 396 6100 or 1-800 327 9074**

Quality Inn Lake Cecile (£)
Budget option with central location close to shopping and dining: 222 rooms; lakeshore site, pool and watersports.
✉ **4944 W Irlo Bronson Memorial Highway/US192**
☎ **(407) 396 4455 or 1-800 864 4855**

Ramada Inn Resort Maingate (££)
Full-service resort with 391

rooms on Walt Disney World Resort's doorstep. Pools, basketball courts, tennis and restaurant.

✉ **2950 Reedy Creek Boulevard** ☎ **(407) 396 4466 or 1-800 365 6935**

Wonderland Inn (££)

A welcome – and welcoming – bed and breakfast option. 11 rooms and suites (some with kitchenettes), plus a cottage in a garden setting. Continental breakfast, wine/cheese hour.

✉ **3601 S Orange Blossom Trail** ☎ **(407) 847 2477 or 1-877 847 2477**

Lake Wales
Chalet Suzanne (£££)

26 large and pretty rooms spread around the grounds of a charming country inn. Peace and quiet, friendly and attentive service; very good restaurant (➤ 96).

✉ **3800 Chalet Suzanne Drive (off CR17A, 4½ miles north of Lake Wales)** ☎ **(863) 676 6011 or 1-800 433 6011**

Winter Park
Langford Resort Hotel (££)

Well away from the hustle and the bustle, the family-owned Langford is a Winter Park institution: slightly aged, but homely and friendly with spacious rooms and a pool.

✉ **300 E New England Avenue, Winter Park** ☎ **(407) 644 3400 or 1-800 203 2581**

Walt Disney World Resort and Lake Buena Vista
Wyndham Palace Resort & Spa (£££)

Luxurious and elegant hotel with 1,013 rooms/suites thoughtfully equipped with spa products (➤ 102, panel).

Excellent recreational facilities; children's programmes; gourmet dining at Arthur's 27 (➤ 97).

✉ **1900 Buena Vista Drive** ☎ **(407) 827 2727**

Disney's All-Star Sports, Movies and Music Resorts (££)

Three good value themed resorts; 5,760 rooms, each able to accommodate four adults; good facilities.

✉ **Animal Kingdom Resort Area** ☎ **(407) 934 7639 or 1-800 647 7900**

Disney's BoardWalk Inn and Villas (£££)

Smart New England-style waterfront resort offering 378 rooms and 532 one-, two- and three-bedroom studios and villas sleeping 4–12 adults. Sporting facilities; children's activities; dining and shopping.

✉ **2101 N Epcot Resorts Boulevard** ☎ **(407) 939 5100; reservations (407) 934 7639**

Disney's Port Orleans Resort (£££)

Mid-range Disney hotel with an attractive New Orleans-style setting providing 1,008 rooms in three-storey buildings. Swimming, tennis courts and boating; restaurants.

✉ **2201 Orleans Drive** ☎ **(407) 934 5000; reservations (407) 934 7639**

Fort Wilderness Campground (£)

Woodland camp site offering hook-up facilities and cabins which can sleep six (£££) (➤ 90).

✉ **4510 N Fort Wilderness Trail** ☎ **(407) 824 2900; reservations (407) 934 7639**

Budget Tips

Most hotels offer accommodation in several price ranges. If you are on a budget and the hotel rate offered is at the top end of your limit, always check to see if there is anything cheaper. If you are prepared to take a chance (not advisable in high season), many hotels are prepared to negotiate on the room price if they still have vacancies later in the day (after 6PM or so).

Shopping Districts & Malls

Mall Wonders

The Florida Mall is the biggest shopping experience in Orlando, anchored by outposts of the Saks Fifth Avenue, Sears, JC Penney, Burdines and Dillard's department stores. Popular brand-name fashion boutiques include Gap, The Limited, Benetton and Banana Republic, and there is a well-stocked Warner Bros Studio Store (► 106). If all that shopping works up a hunger, take your pick from 30 refreshment and dining options in the Food Court.

Orlando

The Florida Mall

Central Florida's largest and most popular shopping destination: 250 speciality stores, anchored by five department stores (see panel).

✉ 8001 S Orange Blossom Trail/US441 ☎ (407) 851 6255 🚌 Lynx #42

The Mall at Millenia

Orlando's latest shopping extravaganza boasting 150-plus fashion and specialist stores from Bang & Olufsen to Gucci via Gap, Neiman Marcus and a selection of eateries.

✉ 4200 Conroy Road (at I-4) ☎ (407) 363 3555

The Mercado

A landmark tower sprouts above this Mediterranean-style marketplace. Some 60 speciality shops and restaurants set around an open-air courtyard with occasional live entertainment.

✉ 8445 International Drive ☎ (407) 345 9337 🚌 I-Ride, Lynx #42

Orlando Fashion Square Mall

Among the 165 boutiques and shops are branches of Sears, Burdines, JC Penney and Dillard's department stores.

✉ 3201 E Colonial Drive/SR50 ☎ (407) 896 1131

Pointe*Orlando

Up-market shopping and entertainment complex on I-Drive anchored by a branch of the FAO Schwartz department store. Mega book and music stores.

✉ 9101 International Drive ☎ (407) 248 2838 🚌 I-Ride, Lynx #42

Around Orlando

Kissimmee

Old Town Kissimmee

Around 70 souvenir stores, boutiques and gift shops, plus restaurants and amusement rides (► 60).

✉ 5770 W Irlo Bronson Memorial Highway/US192 ☎ (407) 396 4888

Winter Park

Park Avenue

An attractive downtown shopping district in the north Orlando suburb of Winter Park. Assorted boutiques, galleries, gifts and restaurants (► 66).

✉ Park Avenue (at New York Avenue) ☎ (407) 644 8281

Walt Disney World Resort and Lake Buena Vista

Crossroads at Lake Buena Vista

Small shopping and dining complex at the entrance to Walt Disney World, with a branch of the Goodings supermarket chain.

✉ 12541 SR535 (opposite Hotel Plaza Boulevard) ☎ (407) 827 7300

Downtown Disney Marketplace

A fun place to shop and catch the breeze off the lake. Souvenirs, resortwear and World of Disney, the biggest Disney merchandise store in the world (► 106). Also restaurants, snack stops and boat hire from Cap'n Jack's Marina.

✉ Buena Vista Drive ☎ (407) 828 3858

Discount Outlets & Bargain Stores

Orlando

Belz Designer Outlet Centre

Just south of Belz (► below), designer fashion bargains from Esprit, DKNY, Off 5th-Saks Fifth Avenue, and others. Also Fila sportswear, china from Villeroy & Boch, jewellery and household appliances.

✉ 5211 International Drive
☎ (407) 352 9611 🚍 I-Ride, Lynx #8, 42

Belz Factory Outlet World

Two full-scale malls and four annexes containing 170-plus outlet stores selling cut-price clothing, footwear, sporting goods and accessories (► panel).

✉ 5401 W Oakridge Road
☎ (407) 352 9611 🚍 I-Ride, Lynx #8, 42

Orlando Premium Outlets

A Mediterranean village setting for 110 stores including Banana Republic, Polo Ralph Lauren, Tommy Hilfiger and Verdace. savings of 25–65 per cent.

✉ 8200 Vineland Avenue
☎ (407) 238 7787 🚍 I-Ride

Sports Dominator, Inc.

Massive selection of sportswear, shoes and equipment from top names including Adidas, Head, Nike and Prince, with discounts of up to 50 per cent on selected items.

✉ 6464 International Drive
☎ (407) 354 2100 🚍 I-Ride, Lynx #42

Around Orlando

Kissimmee

Kissimmee Value Outlet Shops

Mini factory-outlet mall with 30-plus stores, including Nike, Calvin Klein and Tommy Hilfiger, offering 25–75 per cent discounts.

✉ 4673 West US192 ☎ (407) 396 8900

Sports Dominator, Inc.

A Kissimmee outlet for this well-stocked sports outfitters (► Orlando, above).

✉ 7550 W US192 ☎ (407) 397 4700

Osceola Flea & Farmers Market

Sprawling 900-booth flea market (Fri–Sun) specialising in souvenirs, dubious antiques and collectables. Also fresh local produce.

✉ 2801 E Irlo Bronson Memorial Highway/US192
☎ (407) 846 2811

Sanford

Flea World

America's largest weekend market under one roof (Fri–Sun): 1,700 dealer booths and thousands of bargains on souvenirs, toys, household items and unbelievable tat.

✉ US17-92 (4 miles southeast of I-4/Exit 50) ☎ (407) 330 1792

Walt Disney World Resort and Lake Buena Vista

Lake Buena Vista Factory Stores

Over 30 factory-direct outlet stores and a food court. Look out for 20–75 per cent off retail prices from the likes of Reebok, Liz Claiborne, Lee and Wrangler jeans from the VF-Factory Outlet, and the OshKosh B'Gosh Superstore.

✉ 15591 S Apopka-Vineland Road/SR535 (2 miles south of I-4/Exit 27) ☎ (407) 238 9301

Bargain Belz

Resembling a giant shopping theme park at the top of International Drive, Belz is a magnet for thrifty shoppers. Bargain-hunters will find discounts of up to 75 per cent off retail prices on an enormous range of goods. Obviously, few items come that dramatically discounted, but there are considerable savings to be had on top brand products from Bally, Converse, Foot Locker, Guess?, Levi Strauss, OshKosh B'Gosh, Sunglass Hut, Van Heusen and many more.

Souvenirs

The Great Merchandise Heist

If theme park admission were not enough to lighten your wallet, dozens of alluring merchandise outlets make it easy to spend a second unscheduled fortune on souvenirs. One tip is to make a deal with children beforehand about what they can expect to take home (a T-shirt, a stuffed toy, a pair of Mickey Mouse ears etc) and stick to it. Visitors to Walt Disney World Resort can also save valuable sightseeing time by avoiding the theme park stores and visiting the one-stop World of Disney superstore.

Orlando

Bargain World

Huge selection of cut-price Disney, MGM and Florida souvenir T-shirts, plus sportswear, swimwear and beach accessories.
✉ **6454 International Drive**
☎ **(407) 345 8772** ✉ **8520 International Drive** ☎ **(407) 352 0214** 🚌 **I-Ride, Lynx #42**

The Universal Studios Store

Toy and souvenir store packed with Universal merchandise from Woody Woodpecker pyjamas to cuddly Curious Georges.
✉ **Universal CityWalk, 6000 Universal Boulevard** ☎ **(407) 363 8000**

Warner Bros Studio Store

Shelves piled high with cuddly and collectable souvenirs of Bugs Bunny and rest of the Loony Tunes crowd. Clothing, toys and accessories in all guises.
✉ **Victorian Court/Unit 1013, The Florida Mall, 8001 S Orange Blossom Trail/US441** ☎ **(407) 851 6255** 🚌 **Lynx #42**

Around Orlando

Kissimmee

Bargain World

Two Kissimmee locations for Bargain World's discounted souvenirs and fashions (▶ Orlando above).
✉ **5781 W US192 (west of I-4)** ☎ **(407) 396 7778** ✉ **7586 W US192 (east of I-4)** ☎ **(407) 396 7199**

Titusville/Merritt Island

Space Shop

Don't blow the entire souvenir budget on Disney, the Kennedy Space Center's souvenir shop is full of unusual mementoes. Astronaut food is a favourite, plus posters and T-shirts.
✉ **Kennedy Space Center, SR405** ☎ **(407) 452 2121**

Theme Park Outlets

Remaindered souvenir merchandise from Orlando's theme parks provides bargain (50–75 per cent) pickings for canny shoppers.
✉ **Kissimmee Value outlet Shops, 4673 W Irlo Bronson Memorial Highway/US192** ☎ **(407) 390 7803**

Walt Disney World Resort and Lake Buena Vista

The Art of Disney

The place to find Disney posters, animation art, glossy art books and children's story books. Also at Disney-MGM Studios.
✉ **Downtown Disney Marketplace, Buena Vista Drive** ☎ **(407) 828 3058**

Once Upon a Toy

16,000sq feet of Disney themed merchandised plus top toy marque Hasbro of Mr Potato man fame.
✉ **Downtown Disney Marketplace, Lane buena Vista Drive** ☎ **(407) 934 7745**

World of Disney

The world's largest Disney superstore. Just about the full range of Disney merchandise from adults and children's clothing to toys, jewellery and trinkets. Kids and kitsch-crazy adults can blow the entire budget on Minnie Mouse slippers and Tigger baby-gros (▶ panel).
✉ **Downtown Disney Marketplace, Buena Vista Drive** ☎ **(407) 828 3058**

Miscellaneous

Orlando

Beanytoyworld Orlando Superstore

Florida's largest selection of Ty products acts like a magnet for collectors and children (of all ages). Fans can even check out what's on offer in advance over the internet at www.beanytoyworld.com.

✉ **5490 International Drive**
☎ **(407) 352 4636 or 1-800 728 2618** 🚌 **I-Ride, Lynx #42**

Sci-Fi City

The world's largest science fiction store is bursting at the proverbial seams with books, comics, games, figurines and T-shirts galore. Worth a trip for all you sci-fi buffs out there.

✉ **6006 E Colonial Drive**
☎ **(407) 282 2292**

Sound Shop

Stock up on affordable sounds and entertainment from Sound Shop's catalogue of CDs, tapes, movie and music videos, and DVDs.

✉ **Pointe*Orlando (suite 314), 9109 International Drive**
☎ **(407) 363 9882 or 1-800 251**
🚌 **I-Ride, Lynx #42**

World of Denim

Stock up on the top US brand name jeans and casual wear from Levi's, Guess?, DKNY, No Fear, and Timberland among others.

✉ **8255 International Drive**
☎ **(407) 345 0263** 🚌 **I-Ride, Lynx #42** ✉ **5210 W Irlo Bronson Memorial Highway, Kissimmee** ☎ **(407) 390 4561**

Around Orlando

Cocoa Beach

Ron Jon Surf Shop

A local institution in this lively seaside town (▶ 68–9). Nine acres of cool surfie beach gear, sand sculptures, board or in-line skate rental and café. Open 24 hours.

✉ **4151 N Atlantic Avenue/A1A (near junction with SR520)**
☎ **(407) 799 8888**

Kissimmee

Shell World

Florida's oldest and largest retailer of seashells, coral and nautical knick-knacks: 50,000 shells from around the globe from less than a dollar to valuable collectables.

✉ **4727 W Irlo Bronson Memorial Highway/US192**
☎ **(407) 396 9000**

Walt Disney World and Lake Buena Vista

Disney's Days of Christmas

It is 25 December all year round at this Christmassy store laden with yule-themed gifts and decorations. Mickey, Minnie, Winnie the Pooh and other favourite Disney characters are all dressed up and ready for the festivities.

✉ **Downtown Disney Marketplace, Buena Vista Drive**
☎ **(407) 828 3058**

Wyland Galleries of Florida

Marine paintings, sculpture and prints from one of the world's leading environmental artists famous for his giant 'whaling wall murals'.

✉ **671 W Front Street, Celebration** ☎ **(407) 827 1110**
✉ **Disney's BoardWalk, 2101 N Epcot Resorts Boulevard**
☎ **(407) 566 1245**

Antiquing

Antiques-fanciers will find a few browsing spots around Orlando. East of Kissimmee, almost a dozen small antiques and collectables stores gather around New York Avenue in downtown St Cloud's quiet historic district. For more up-market pickings, try the smart antiques shops and galleries on Park Avenue in the prosperous Orlando suburb of Winter Park (▶ 66). But the best antiquing opportunity around is downtown Mount Dora (▶ 54).

Alternative Attractions

Theme Park Survival Tips

The chief rule is: don't overdo it. Tired, overwrought children are bad company, so tailor your stay to their energy levels. Rent a stroller so that young children can always hitch a ride, and take plenty of short breaks. Walt Disney World Resort or Universal Studio Escape guests staying close by might consider making an early start, returning to the hotel for a rest and a swim, and revisiting the park in the cool of the evening (get a handstamp to allow readmittance). Be warned: many of the thrill rides are limited to passengers measuring 44 inches (3ft 8in, or 1.12m) or more.

Orlando is all about children, but there are a few options other than the theme parks for younger visitors.

Orlando

Fun Spot Action Park

Multi-level, action-packed family attraction with go-karting, bumper cars and boats. Fairground-style rides such as the ferris wheel and kiddie rides. Also a massive games arcade.

✉ 5551 Del Verde Way (off International Drive) ☎ (407) 363 3867 🕙 Mon–Fri noon–midnight; Sat and Sun 10AM–midnight

Magical Midway

Another I-Drive family fun zone offering the full package of extreme go-kart tracks with corkscrew turns and wacky elevations, laser tag, bumper boats and cars, plus a giant slide.

✉ Pointe*Orlando, 7001 International Drive ☎ (407) 370 5353 🕙 Sun–Thu 12–10, Fri 12–12 🚌 I-Ride, Lynx #42

Orlando Science Center

A fun state-of-the-art science museum with dozens of interactive exhibits, film shows, a planetarium and 3-D laser shows (➤ 35).

✉ 777 E Princeton Street (I-4/Exit 85) ☎ (407) 514 2000 or 1-800 672 4386 🕙 Tue–Thu 9–5, Fri–Sat 9–9, Sun 12–5. Closed Thanksgiving and Christmas

Skull Kingdom

Step through a giant skull into this haunting family attraction. Spooky, interactive exhibits augmented by live actors and special effects culminating in the Ghoulish Face Painting Gallery.

Recommended for age 8 and up.

✉ 5933 American Way (off International Drive) ☎ (407) 354 1564 🕙 Daily 12–2

WonderWorks

A Spielberg-inspired interactive games attraction boasting 100-plus exhibits from earthquake and hurricane simulators to virtual hang-gliding and laser tag. A favourite is a design-your-own roller coaster site.

✉ Pointe*Orlando, 9067 International Drive ☎ (407) 351 8800 🕙 Daily 9–midnight 🚌 I-Ride, Lynx #42

Around Orlando

Clearwater Beach

Sea Screamer

A day trip from orlando (approx 90 mins west via I-4), Clearwater is renowned for glorious beaches and dolphin cruises. Here the 73ft, twin-turbo Sea Screamer (the world's biggest speedboat) combines a gentle harbour cruise with a blast out into the Gulf of Mexico that guarantees thrills, dolphin sightings and a probable drenching.

✉ Clearwater Beach Marina ☎ (727) 447 7200 🕙 Spring–autumn daily at noon, 2PM, 4PM; Jun to mid-Sep also 6PM

Kissimmee

Green Meadows Petting Farm

Farmyard fun for young children with pony rides and lots of animals to meet and pet (➤ 55).

✉ 1368 S Poinciana Boulevard ☎ (407) 846 0770 🕙 Daily 9:30–5:30

Horse World
Saddle up for a gentle nature trail or an excursion for more experienced riders through a 750-acre woodland preserve. Pony rides for little children.

✉ **3705 S Poinciana Boulevard** ☎ **(407) 847 4343** 🕐 **Daily from 9AM**

The Ice Factory
New ice-skating centre with two rinks and skating lessons. Skate rental and pro-shop, plus a children's play area, snack bar and video arcade.

✉ **2221 Partin Settlement Road** ☎ **(407) 933 4259** 🕐 **Daily 6AM–midnight**

Kissimmee Family Aquatic Center
A bargain alternative to the expensive water parks, this family pool is a great place to splash around, play on the scaled-down waterslide and lounge in the sun, all for only a couple of dollars.

✉ **2204 Denn John Lane** ☎ **(407) 870 7665** 🕐 **Spring Break (late Mar) to end Sep; check schedules. Closed winter and Mon**

Pirate's Cove and Pirate's Island Adventure Golf
There are two 18-hole miniature golf courses with a buccaneering theme at each of these locations.

✉ **4330 W Vine Street/US192** ☎ **(407) 396 4660** ✉ **2845 Florida Plaza Boulevard** ☎ **(407) 396 7484** 🕐 **Daily 9AM–11:30PM**

Lake Monroe
Central Florida Zoological Park
Animal encounters in a Florida woodland setting among the live oaks and Spanish moss. The residents include big cats, monkeys, birds and reptiles. There are picnic areas and an animal petting corner.

✉ **US17-92 (south of I-4/Exit 52 towards Sanford)** ☎ **(407) 323 4450** 🕐 **Daily 9–5, except Thanksgiving and Christmas**

Ocala
Don Garlits Automotive Attractions
A popular outing for boy (or girl) racers – and their dads and mums. There's 46,000 square feet of automotive excellence from muscle cars, hot rods and race cars to vintage Fords and a motor racing hall of fame.

✉ **13700 SW 16th Avenue (55 miles N of Orlando)** ☎ **(352) 245 8661** 🕐 **Daily 9–5**

Juniper Creek Canoe Run
Great for older children. The seven-mile canoe trail runs through the Ocala National Forest (▶ 62) and takes around four hours. Canoes can be rented in advance.

✉ **Juniper Springs Recreation Area, SR40 (22 miles east of Silver Springs), Ocala National Forest** ☎ **(352) 625 2802** 🕐 **Mon–Fri 9–noon, Sat–Sun 8–noon**

Walt Disney World Resort and Lake Buena Vista
DisneyQuest
Five floors of state-of-the-art interactive adventures and virtual reality experiences for all ages. Dodge the realistic virtual dinosaurs, design a roller-coaster and 'fly' Aladdin's magic carpet.

✉ **Downtown Disney West Side** ☎ **(407) 828 4600** 🕐 **Daily 10:30AM–midnight**

Southern Belles at Cypress Gardens
Drifting around the floral displays at Cypress Gardens (▶ 18, 52), like errant extras from the set of *Gone With the Wind*, the park's ringleted and crinolined trademark Southern Belles are many a little girl's dream. The Junior Belle Boutique, in the Southern Crossroads area, will transform junior misses (aged 3–12) into replica Southern Belles with make-up, hair-styling and a photograph to take home (additional charge).

Beyond the Theme Parks

Citrus Country
Thousands of acres of Central Florida are planted with citrus trees, but visitors rarely get a chance to stop and explore the groves. During winter (Nov–Apr), Ivey Groves Fresh Citrus, 2220 Boggy Creek Road, Kissimmee (☎ (407) 348 4757) offer daily orchard tours, and a chance to pick your own citrus fruits and sample free juices. At the Florida Citrus Tower (US 27 at Clermont, 23 miles west of Orlando), visitors are whisked up the 226ft observation tower for an unparalleled view of the groves below, which can also be visited on foot or by tram tour.

Orlando
Rise and Float Balloon Tours
A bird's-eye view of Central Florida from theme parks to citrus groves. Balloons depart from Mystery Fun House (► 108). 'For lovers only' private flights available.
- ✉ 5767 Major Boulevard (off I-Drive, opposite Universal Orlando) ☎ (407) 352 8191 🕐 Daily, weather permitting

Around Orlando

Clermont
Laneridge Winery and Vineyards
Florida's largest and award-winning winery offers tours and tastings of red, white, rosé and sparkling wines.
- ✉ 19239 US27 North ☎ (352) 394 8627 or 1-800 768 9463 🕐 Mon–Sat 10–5, Sun 11–5

Daytona
Daytona USA
Take a trip to the 'World Center of Racing' visitor centre at the famous Daytona Speedway. Racing memorabilia, excellent interactive displays and games, merchandise store and guided track tours.
- ✉ 1801 W International Speedway Boulevard/US92 (I-4/Exit 57, 50 miles E of Orlando) ☎ (386) 947 6800 🕐 Daily 9–5

Kissimmee
Aquatic Wonders Boat Trips
Two-hour and half-day boat trips on Lake Tohopekaliga (► 61). Fishing trips, birding and sunset cruises.
- ✉ 101 E Lakeshore Boulevard ☎ (407) 846 2814 🕐 Daily from 9AM, by appointment

Boggy Creek Airboat Rides
Half-hour airboat trips into the Central Florida wetlands explore 10 miles of sawgrass and natural creeks looking for wildlife. Nighttime 'gator hunts by arrangement.
- ✉ East Lake Fish Camp, 3702 Big Bass Road (off Boggy Creek Road) ☎ (407) 348 4676 🕐 Daily 9AM–dusk

Kissimmee Rodeo
Kissimmee's cowboys and cowgirls compete in trials of skill and daring (► 60).
- ✉ Kissimmee Sports Arena, 958 S Hoagland Boulevard ☎ (407) 933 0020 🕐 Fri 8–10PM

Warbird Adventures, Inc.
Take to the skies in T-6/Harvard World War II fighter-trainer for an aerobatic adventure or gentle sightseeing flight.
- ✉ 233 N Hoagland Boulevard ☎ (407) 870 7366 ot 1-800 386 1593 🕐 Daily 9–sunset

Walt Disney World Resort and Lake Buena Vista
Richard Petty Driving Experience
Ride with a pro or drive a 630hp NASCAR stock car down the backstretch at speeds of up to 145mph.
- ✉ Walt Disney Speedway ☎ (407) 939 0130 or 1-800 237 3889 🕐 Daily 8–5 (extended in summer)

Sanford
Rivership Romance
Riverboat lunch and Friday and Saturday night dinner-dance cruises on Lake Monroe and St Johns River. Popular with an older crowd.
- ✉ 433 N Palmetto Avenue ☎ (407) 321 5091 or 1-800 423 7401 🕐 Daily 8:30–5:30

Sports

Fishing

Orlando

Bass Challenger Guide Services, Inc
Full- and half-day fishing trips with all equipment and transportation provided.
✉ PO Box 679155 ☎ (407) 273 8045 or 1-800 241 5314
🕐 Daily, by arrangement

Kissimmee

A #1 Bass Guide Service
Fully rigged bass boats and tackle for half-, full-day and nighttime fishing trips.
✉ PO Box 421257, Kissimmee ☎ (352) 394 3660 or 1-800 707 5463 🕐 Daily, by arrangement

Golf

► 68–9.

Horse-riding

Orlando

Grand Cypress Equestrian Center
A wide variety of lessons and programmes, English and Western trail rides at this up-market hotel resort.
✉ Grand Cypress Resort, One Grand Cypress Boulevard ☎ (407) 239 1981 or 1-800 835 7377
🕐 Daily 8–5

Kissimmee

Horse World Riding Stables
Woodland trails for experienced and novice riders (► 108).
✉ 3705 S Poinciana Boulevard ☎ (407) 847 4343 🕐 Daily from 9AM

Walt Disney World Resort and Lake Buena Vista

Trailblaze Corral
Trail rides through the Fort Wilderness countryside (riders must be aged 9 or more). Also pony rides for little children. (► 90)
✉ Disney's Fort Wilderness Resort, 4510 N Fort Wilderness Trail ☎ (407) 939 7529
🕐 Daily 10–5

Tennis

Orlando

Orlando Tennis Center
A good downtown budget option with 16 courts and good facilities.
✉ 649 W Livingstone Street ☎ (407) 246 2162 🕐 Mon–Fri 8–10, Sat 8–8, Sun 8–6

Kissimmee

Orange Lake Country Club & Resort
Sixteen well-priced courts close to Disney; advance reservations are not always necessary.
✉ 8505 W Irlo Bronson Memorial Highway/US192 ☎ (407) 239 1050 🕐 Daily

Walt Disney World Resort and Lake Buena Vista

Disney's Racquet Club
State-of-the-art clay courts, private and group lessons, tennis ball machines, or sign up at Players Without Partners.
✉ Disney's Contemporary Resort ☎ (407) 939 7529
🕐 Daily

Watersports

Orlando

Buena Vista Water Sports/Dave's Ski School
Water-ski lessons, Jet Ski and competition ski boat rentals, and tube rides for groups (see panel).
✉ 13245 Lake Bryan Drive ☎ (407) 239 6939 🕐 Daily

Watersports at Walt Disney World Resort
Walt Disney World Resort's numerous lakes and lagoons are ideal for messing about on the water. Most of the hotels have waterfrontage and marinas where guests can rent a variety of small sail boats, jet boats, watersprites and pedal boats. There is water-skiing from the Fort Wilderness marina, parasailing from the Contemporary Resort, and canoeing along scenic canals from the Fort Wilderness, Caribbean Beach, Dixie Landings and Port Orleans marinas.

Spectator Sports

Spring Training

While most of the country shivers in grim winter temperatures, sunny Central Florida is the ideal location for the nation's top baseball teams to get in shape for the forthcoming playing season. During Feburary and March, fans can catch friendly games and practice sessions from the Houston Astros at Kissimmee, and the Atlanta Braves at Disney's Wide World of Sports Complex. Elsewhere in Central Florida, the Detroit Tigers train at Lakeland and the Cleveland Indians at Winter Haven.

American Football

Orlando Predators

Aspiring local Arena Football League competitors. Check listings in the local papers for details of upcoming games.
✉ **TD Waterhouse Centre, 4901 Vineland Road #150** ☎ **(407) 648 4444**

Baseball

Orlando
Orlando Rays
The Florida Marlins are the state's only major league baseball team, but the 'Double A' Rays perform at Wide World of Sports Apr–Sep.
✉ **Walt Disney world Resort** ☎ **(407) 934 7007**

Kissimmee
Osceola County Stadium & Sports Complex
Spring training home of the Houston Astros (▶ panel) and host to many amateur and professional baseball events throughout the year.
✉ **1000 Bill Beck Boulevard (off E US192)** ☎ **(407) 933 5400**

Basketball

Orlando Magic
Downtown TD Waterhouse Centre is home to the local Eastern Division NBA contenders when they are in town. Season Oct to Apr/May, reservations advised.
✉ **TD Waterhouse Centre, 8701 Maitland Summit Boulevard** ☎ **(407) 896 2442 or 1-800 338 0005** ❓ **Tickets from Ticketmaster** ☎ **1-800 4NBA TIX**

Orlando Miracle
When the Magic are taking a summer break, the Miracle women's NBA professionals provide fun family sporting entertainment.
✉ **TD Waterhouse Centre, 8701 Maitland Summit Boulevard** ☎ **(407) 916 9622**

Golf

PGA Events
Home to 30 PGA Tour pros and 11 LPGA pros, Orlando is Florida's golfing capital. Local courses host two annual PGA events: in Mar, the Bay Hill Invitational is played at the Arnold Palmer Golf Academy, 9000 Bay Hill Boulevard, Orlando ☎ (407) 876 5362; in Oct, Disney offer a million-dollar purse for the National Car Rental Golf Classic ☎ (407) 939 4653.

Motor Racing

Daytona International Speedway
Home to the famous Daytona 500 and Speed Weeks race programme (Feb), plus the Bike Week (Mar) and Bikeoctober (Oct) motorcyle events.
✉ **1801 W International Speedway Boulevard** ☎ **(386) 253 RACE (7223)**

Sports Complex

Disney's Wide World of Sports Complex
Transforming Orlando into a major sporting venue at a stroke, Disney's spectacular 200-acre sports complex boasts world-class facilities for more than 30 sports, a speedway, and hosts national and international events.
✉ **Lake Buena Vista** ☎ **(407) 934 7007** 🕐 **Daily 10–5 and special events**

Dinner Shows

Orlando
Mark Two Dinner Theater
Expect a superior cast from Orlando's only professional theatre that boasts membership of the Actor's Equity Association. Full-scale broadway shows and all-you-can-eat buffet.

✉ 3376 Edgewater Drive
☎ (407) 83 6275 ⏰ Nightly

Pirate's Dinner Adventure
Yo ho ho and a suitably piratical dinner show with a motley crew of entertainers, stunt men and a post-show Buccaneer Bash.

✉ 6400 Carrier Drive (off International Drive) ☎ (407) 248 0590 or 1-800 866 2469 ⏰ Nightly

Sleuths Mystery Dinner Shows
Solve a whodunnit between courses at this small dinner attraction. Entertaining action with a comedy angle and plenty of red herrings, but dinner is a rather long-winded affair for those attending the second show.

✉ 7508 Universal Boulevard
☎ (407) 363 1985 ⏰ Nightly

Around Orlando

Kissimmee
Arabian Nights
A glittering equestrian spectacular, this is one of Orlando's main dinner attractions, with over $5 million-worth of prime horseflesh and enough glitz to rival Las Vegas. Good family entertainment and a real treat for horse-mad kids.

✉ 6225 W Irlo Bronson Memorial Highway/US192 (GM 8) ☎ (407) 239 9223 or 1-800 553 6116 ⏰ Nightly

Capone's
An intimate 1930s speakeasy is the setting for this gangsters-and-molls comedy musical show. Good tunes, the small cast throws itself into the dance numbers with enthusiasm, and Bunny the Cigarette Girl steals the show.

✉ 4740 W Irlo Bronson Memorial Highway/US192 (GM 12.5) ☎ (407) 397 2378 or 1-800 220 8428 ⏰ Nightly

Medieval Times
An evening of medieval spectator sports as dashing knights take part in action-packed horseback games of skill and daring, jousting and sword fights.

✉ 4510 W Irlo Bronson Memorial Highway/US192 (GM 14.5) ☎ (407) 239 0214 or 1-800 229 8300 ⏰ Nightly

Walt Disney World Resort and Lake Buena Vista
Hoop-Dee Doo Musical Revue
Enormously popular Disney country-style hoe-down with sing-along tunes and a good all-you-can-eat barbecue banquet. Three shows nightly; advance reservations a must.

✉ Disney's Fort Wilderness Resort, 4510 N Fort Wilderness Trail ☎ (407) 939 3463 ⏰ Nightly

Soulfire Theatre and Dinner Experience
Be part of the show as guests are co-opted into the action at a wild migh school graduation class reunion. Music, dance, karaoke and much more.

✉ Lake Buena Vista Factory Stores, 15609 Apopka Vineland Road ☎ (407) 465 1886 ⏰ Nightly

The Bottom Line
Dinner shows are enormously popular, but they are not cheap. The average price for dinner (including unlimited wine, beer and non-alcoholic drinks) and a show is around $45 per adult. And, let's be honest, dinner theatres are not in the business of gourmet dining. Food is generally plentiful, but indifferent, tepid and occasionally inedible. The trick is to ignore promising menu descriptions and pick out the show most suited to your group of family or friends.

113

Live Music, Entertainment & Sports Bars

Stargazing

For a rather less conventional night out, the Orlando Science Center (▶ 35) invites stargazers to survey the universe through Florida's largest publicly accessible refractor telescope on Friday and Saturday evenings. On the same evenings, the Center also features laser light shows to rock music soundtracks and 3-D special effects in the world's largest Digistar II Planetarium, the CineDome (information, ☎ (407) 514 2114 or 1-888 672 4386).

Orlando

Friday's Front Row Sports Grill

Satellite sporting entertainment on tap, all-American menu and games room.

✉ 8126 International Drive
☎ (407) 363 1414
🕐 Daily until 2AM
🚍 I-Ride, Lynx #42

Howl at the Moon Saloon

Duelling pianos, sing-a-long rock 'n' roll favourites, audience participation and party atmosphere. Minimum age 21.

✉ 55 W Church Street
☎ (407) 841 9118 🕐 Nightly until 2AM

Pointe*Orlando

After dark entertainment at a choice of restaurants, clubs and a multi-screen cinema with an IMAX 3-D theatre.

✉ 9101 International Drive (at Republic Drive) ☎ (407) 248 2838 🕐 Daily 🚍 I-Ride, Lynx #42

Sak Comedy Lab

Best live comedy venue in Orlando. Award-winning improvisational shows at this downtown location.

✉ 380 W Amelia Street
☎ (407) 648 0001 🕐 Check schedules

Universal CityWalk

Universal's dining and entertainment zone includes the Motown Café, CityJazz, Bob Marley – A Tribute to Freedom, the NASCAR café and Pat O'Brien's Irish bar, as well as a Hard Rock Café and a Hard Rock Live music venue.

✉ Universal Orlando, 1000 Universal Boulevard
☎ (407) 363 8000
🕐 Nightly

Walt Disney World Resort and Lake Buena Vista

Cirque du Soleil-La Naba

Created exclusively for Walt Disney World by the world-renowned Cirque du Soleil, La Naba is more an experience than a show. Avant-garde choreography meets Broadway spectacle and fantastical sets. There is live music, breathtaking circus skills and the requsite dose of whimsy as cast captivate audiences of all ages.

✉ Downtown Disney West Side ☎ (407) 939 7600 🕐 Thu–Mon at 6PM and 9PM

Copa Banana

Premiere Disney nightspot with a Caribbean flavour offering dancing, karaoke, and satellite TV for sports events.

✉ Disney's Dolphin Resort, 1500 Epcot Boulevard ☎ (407) 934 4000 🕐 Nightly

Disney's BoardWalk

Live dance music from the 1940s to the 1990s at Atlantic Dance; duelling grand pianos at Jellyrolls; also the ESPN Club sports bar (minimum age 21 at Atlantic Dance and Jellyrolls).

✉ 2101 N Epcot Resorts Boulevard ☎ (407) 939 5100 🕐 Nightly

House of Blues

Restaurant-cum-live music venue featuring blues, R&B, jazz and country. Occassional top name performers (check schedules).

✉ Downtown Disney West Side ☎ (407) 934 2583 🕐 Mon–Thu 7:30–2AM, Fri–Sat 8–2AM, Sun 9–3AM

Nightclubs &
Discotheques

Orlando

Backstage at the Rosen
Live bands and DJs playing hits from the 1970s through to the present day at International Drive's only nightclub without a cover charge.

✉ **Clarion Plaza Hotel, 9700 International Drive** ☎ **(407) 996 9700 ext 1684** 🕐 **Nightly until 2AM** 🚌 **I-Ride, Lynx #42**

Cairo
This is the place where the locals go to let their hair down. High energy dance, disco and reggae music in three separate areas.

✉ **22 S Magnolia Avenue** ☎ **(407) 422 3595** 🕐 **Wed–Sun 10PM–3AM**

The Groove
Featuring state-of-the-art sound and lighting, DJ Club and Dance mixes plus occasional live shows. Three of the seven bars are themed 'mood' rooms where guests can chat over expensive cocktails.

✉ **Universal CityWalk, 6000 Universal Boulevard** ☎ **(407) 363 8000** 🕐 **Nightly until 2AM**

Matrix
Orlando's largest dance floor, a multi-million dollar light show and changing menu of DJ selected Top 40, techno, Eurotrance and breakout sounds all conveniently located on I-Drive. Good for groups.

✉ **Pointe* Orlando, 9101 International Drive, Suite 2300** ☎ **(407) 370 3700** 🕐 **Nightly until 3am** 🚌 **I-Ride, Lynx #42**

Tabu
A downtown venue for clubbers who prefer a more sophisticated SoBe (that's South Beach, Miami) atmosphere. State-of-the-art sound system, sushi bar, private VIP rooms with views of the dance floor on the upper level. Sunday night is Latin night. Min. age 21.

✉ **46 N Orange Avenue** ☎ **(407) 648 8363** 🕐 **Tue–Sat until 3am and Sun**

Around Orlando

Walt Disney World Resort and Lake Buena Vista
Atlantic Dance Hall
A reliable, popular and eclectic dance club in the Disney's BoardWalk entertainment zone (▶ 114). Live music from Thu to Sat.

✉ **2101 N Epcot Resorts Boulevard** ☎ **(407) 939 2444** 🕐 **Nightly from 9PM**

Laughing Kookaburra Good Time Bar
Popular and often very crowded hotel nightclub with a surprisingly small dance floor. There is live music, contemporary chart hits, speciality cocktails and a good party atmosphere.

✉ **Wyndham Palace Resort & Spa, 1900 Buena Vista Drive** ☎ **(407) 827 3722** 🕐 **Nightly until 2AM**

Pleasure Island
Dedicated to a certain kind of hedonism, Pleasure Island has three discos (8Trax, Mannequins and the Rock-n-Roll Beach Club) and four clubs, including comedy and country and western venues, all crammed into Disney's top nighttime entertainment complex (▶ 89).

✉ **Downtown Disney, E Buena Vista Drive** ☎ **(407) 934 7781** 🕐 **Nightly until 2AM**

It's the Law
Most discotheques and clubs admit under 18s as long as they are accompanied by an adult, though some insist on a minimum age of 21. Florida law prohibits the purchase or consumption of alcohol by anyone under 21. IDs are checked frequently, so any youthful-looking adults would be well advised to carry a passport or similar form of ID showing proof of their age. Everybody (regardless of seniority) must provide proof of age for admission to Pleasure Island.

What's on When

January
Capital One: nationally televised college football game on New Year's Day

February
International Carillon Festival: carillon concerts at Bok Tower Gardens
Silver Spurs Rodeo: major event on the Professional Rodeo Cowboys Association circuit held in Kissimmee
Daytona Speed Weeks: the Daytona 500 and more

March
Cypress Gardens Spring Flower Festival: award-winning floral displays (until May)
Kissimmee Blue Grass Festival: week-long toe-tapping music event
Winter Park Sidewalk Arts Festival: long weekend of art, food, music and activities
Pro Water Ski Tour and Wakeboard Series: waterbatics at the Orlando Water Sports Complex

April
Epcot International Flower & Garden Festival: garden and greenhouse tours, demonstrations and displays

May
Zellwood Sweet Corn Festival: 200,000 corn on the cobs get consumed over the weekend at this family event

June
Florida Film Festival: full-length movies, documentaries and shorts from around the world
Wet 'n Wild Summer Nights Start of summer late night season featuring live entertainment

July
Lake Eola Fireworks at the Fountain: Orlando celebrates the Fourth of July with games, activities and fireworks in Lake Eola Park

August
Cypress Gardens World Precisiion Hang Gliding Tournament: top gliders demonstrate gliding skills.

October
National Car Rental Golf Classic at Walt Disney World Resort top golfers gather for this annual PGA Tour event
Halloween: special events at Cypress Gardens and Universal Orlando's Islands of Adventure
Silver Spurs Rodeo: the cowboys are back in Kissimmee

November
Orlando Magic Season Opener: the Magic open the basketball season
Cypress Gardens Mum (Chrysanthemum) Festival: 2.5 million blooms in spectacular displays
Annual Festival of the Masters: art show at Downtown Disney

December
Cypress Gardens Poinsettia Festival & Garden of Lights: 400,000 lights and 40,000 poinsettias for Christmas
Mickey's Very Merry Christmas Party: celebrations at Magic Kingdom
Christmas in the Park: exhibition of Tiffany glass with seasonal music in downtown Winter Park
SeaWorld Orlando's Rockin' Holiday Nights New Year's Eve New Year's Eve celebrations

Practical Matters

Above: *taxi driver*
Right: *Monument to the States,
Kissimmee*

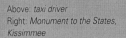

117

TIME DIFFERENCES

GMT	Orlando	Germany	USA (NY)	Netherlands	Spain
12 noon	← 7AM	→ 1PM	← 7AM	→ 1PM	→ 1PM

BEFORE YOU GO

WHAT YOU NEED

● Required
○ Suggested
▲ Not required

	UK	Germany	USA	Netherlands	Spain
Passport (valid for six months from date of entry)/National Identity Card	●	●	▲	●	●
Visa (Waiver form to be completed. Regulations change, please check)	▲	▲	▲	▲	▲
Onward or Return Ticket	●	●	▲	●	●
Health Inoculations (tetanus)	○	○	○	○	○
Health Documentation (reciprocal agreement) (➤ 123, Health)	▲	▲	▲	▲	▲
Travel Insurance	●	●	▲	●	●
Driving Licence (national or International Driving Permit)	●	●	●	●	●
Car Insurance Certificate	○	○	●	○	○
Car Registration Document	●	●	●	●	●

WHEN TO GO

Orlando

▬▬▬ High season
☐ Low season

22°C	23°C	25°C	27°C	27°C	30°C	32°C	32°C	30°C	28°C	25°C	22°C
JAN	FEB	MAR	APR	MAY	JUN	JUL	AUG	SEP	OCT	NOV	DEC
☀	☁	☁	☀	⛅	☁	☁	☁	☁	☁	☀	☀

🌧 Wet   ☁ Cloud   ☀ Sun   ⛅ Sunshine & showers

TOURIST OFFICES

In the UK
Orlando/Kissimmee–St Cloud Tourism Bureau, Inc. Visitor information and a free Orlando/Kissimmee pack of visitor guides to both areas and local map ☎ 020 7233 2305 or 0800 092 2352 (brochure line)

Complete and up-to-date details on attractions, dining, shopping, nightlife and recreation are available from www.orlandoinfo.com/uk and www.floridakiss.com

Visit Florida
For an *Official Florida Holiday Guide* ☎ 01737 644882. Visit Florida also provide a free phone tourist assistance hotline in Florida ☎ 1-800 656 8777. Further information from www.flausa.com

POLICE 911

FIRE 911

AMBULANCE 911

POLICE (NON EMERGENCY) 407/246 2414

WHEN YOU ARE THERE

ARRIVING

International carriers fly direct into Orlando Internatinal Airport, many services involve transfers to and from other US cities. The nearest alternative international gateway for scheduled flights is Tampa, 1½ hours from Orlando; several charter operators serve Orlando Sanford, 20 mins from Orlando.

Orlando International Airport
Kilometres to city centre | **Journey times**

15 kilometres

🚇	N/A
🚌	45 minutes
🚗	30 minutes

Tampa International Airport
Kilometres to city centre | **Journey times**

137 kilometres

🚇	2 hours
🚌	2 hours
🚗	90 minutes

MONEY

An unlimited amount of US dollars can be imported or exported, but amounts of over £10,000 must be reported to US Customs, as should similar amounts of gold. US dollars traveller's cheques ('checks' in America) are accepted as cash in most places (not taxis) as are major credit cards.
Dollar bills come in 1,5, 10, 20, 50, 100 and 500 denominations. Note that all dollar bills are the same size and colour – all greenbacks. One dollar is made up of 100 cents. Coins are of 1 cent (pennies), 5 cents (nickel), 10 cents (dime), 25 cents (quarter) and 1 dollar.

TIME

 Orlando local time is Eastern Standard Time (the same as New York) which is five hours behind Greenwich Mean Time (GMT−5). Daylight saving applies, with clocks one hour ahead between April and October.

CUSTOMS

 YES

There are duty-free allowances for non-US residents over 21 years of age:
Alcohol: spirits (over 22% volume): 1L
Wine: 1L
Cigarettes: 200 *or*
Cigars: 50 *or*
Tobacco: 2kg
Duty-free gifts: $100 provided the stay in US is at least 72 hours and that gift exemption has not been claimed in the previous six months. There are no currency limits.

 NO

Meat or meat products, dairy products, fruits, seeds, drugs, lottery tickets or obscene publications.
Never carry a bag through Customs for anyone else.

CONSULATES/EMBASSIES

UK
☎ (407) 426 7855

Germany
☎ (202) 298 4320
(Washington)

Netherlands
☎ (407) 425 8000

Spain
☎ (305) 446 551
(Miami)

WHEN YOU ARE THERE

TOURIST OFFICES

Official Visitor Centre
● 8723 International Drive, Gala Center (cnr Austrian Row)
Orlando, Florida 32819
☎ (407) 363 5872
🕐 All year 8AM–7PM.

Central Florida Visitors & Convention Bureau
● 1339 Helena Road, Winter Haven
☎ (863) 298 7565 or 1-800 828 7655
🕐 Daily 9–6

Daytona Beach Area Convention & Visitors Centre
● Visitor Information Centre, Daytona USA, 1801 W International Speedway Boulevard
☎ (386) 253 8669 or 1-800 854 1234

Florida's Space Coast Office of Tourism
● 8810 Astronaut Boulevard, Cape Canaveral
☎ (321) 868 1126 or 1-800 93-OCEAN
Information desks at Kennedy Space Center Visitor Complex

Kissimmee – St Cloud Convention & Visitors Bureau
● Visitor Information Centre, 1925 E Irlo Bronson Memorial Highway/US192
☎ (407) 847 5000 or 1-800 333 KISS 🕐 Daily 8–5

Tampa Bay Visitor Information Center
● 615 Channelside Drive
☎ (813) 223 2752
🕐 Daily 9–6

NATIONAL HOLIDAYS

J	F	M	A	M	J	J	A	S	O	N	D
2	1	(1)	(1)	1		1		1	1	2	1

1 Jan	New Year's Day
Jan (third Mon)	Martin Luther King Day
Feb (third Mon)	Washington's Birthday
Mar/Apr	Good Friday
May (last Mon)	Memorial Day
4 Jul	Independence Day
Sep (first Mon)	Labor Day
Oct (second Mon)	Columbus Day
11 Nov	Veterans' Day
Nov (fourth Thu)	Thanksgiving
25 Dec	Christmas Day

Boxing Day is not a public holiday in the US. Some shops open on National Holidays.

OPENING HOURS

○ Shops ● Post Offices
● Offices ◐ Museums
● Banks ◐ Pharmacies

8AM	9AM	10AM	NOON	2PM	3PM	4PM	5PM	6PM

☐ Day ☐ Midday
▨ Evening

There are two all-night pharmacies: Ekered Drugs, 908 Lee Road, and Walgreen Drug Store, International Drive (opposite Wet 'n' Wild). Some shops in malls and on International Drive open until 9PM. Post offices are few and far between; hotels are usually helpful with postal matters. Banks, offices and post offices close on Saturday. Opening times of theme parks vary with seasonal demand. Opening times of museums vary; check with individual museum. Some museums are closed on Monday.

**DRIVE ON THE
RIGHT**

**TOILETS
FREE**

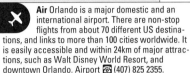

PUBLIC TRANSPORT

Air Orlando is a major domestic and an international airport. There are non-stop flights from about 70 different US destinations, and links to more than 100 cities worldwide. It is easily accessible and within 24km of major attractions, such as Walt Disney World Resort, and downtown Orlando. Airport ☎ (407) 825 2355.

Trains Amtrak trains serve Orlando with four daily trains originating in New York, and Miami, also stopping at Winter Park and Sanford, north of the city, and Kissimmee near Walt Disney World Resort. Amtrak offers an Auto Train overnight service with sleepers, which conveys passengers with their cars and vans, and runs daily between Lorton, Va and Sanford, Fl. For general information ☎ 1-800 872 7245 (toll-free).

Buses Greyhound lines serve Orlando from many centres in the US: within the metropolitan area local buses provide a good service, notably Mears Transportation, which serves the airport and most of Orlando's main attractions and hotels. Greyhound bus ☎ 1-800 231 2222. For excursions around the area and to the major attractions, tour companies offer diverse itineraries or can customise trips for groups.

Urban Transport Besides taxi and limousine service to anywhere in the Greater Orlando area, the city's Lynx bus system provides economical public transportation around Orlando ☎ (407) 841 8240. Bus stops are marked with a 'paw' print of a Lynx cat. The I-ride buses serve International Drive, with stops every 5–10 minutes ☎ (407) 248 9590. The stops are marked 'I-RIDE' at each Lynx bus stop.

CAR RENTAL

Rates are very competitive. Take an unlimited mileage deal, collision damage waiver and adequate (more than minimal) insurance. There is a surcharge on drivers under 25 and the minimum age is often 21 (sometimes 25). Expect to pay by credit card.

TAXIS

Cabs are plentiful in Orlando, but they are not accustomed to being hailed down in the street. Hotels are the best places to find a cab. If money is no object, limousine transport can be easily arranged through your hotel's guest services desk.

DRIVING

Speed limit on interstate highways **55–70mph**

Speed limits on main roads: **55mph**

Speed limits on urban roads: **20–30mph**. All speed limits are strictly enforced.

Must be worn by drivers and front-seat passengers. Children under four must use child safety seats; older children must use a safety seat or seat belt.

Y

There are tough drinking and driving laws. Limit: 0.08 per cent of alcohol in blood.

Fuel (*gasoline*), is cheaper in America than in Europe. It is sold in American gallons (five American gallons equal 18 litres), and comes in three grades, all unleaded. Many gas stations have automatic vending machines that accept notes and major credit cards.

If you break down pull over, raise the bonnet (hood), switch on the hazard lights, and call the rental company or the breakdown number, which should be displayed on or near the dashboard. For added security, several major rental car agencies (including Alamo, Avis and Hertz) are now offering clients the option to rent an in-car mobile phone.

CENTIMETRES

INCHES

PERSONAL SAFETY

Orlando is not generally a dangerous place but to help prevent crime and accidents:

- Never open your hotel room door unless you know who is there. If in doubt call hotel security.
- Place valuables in a safety deposit box.
- Always lock your front and/or patio doors when in the room and when leaving. Use the safety chain/lock for security.
- When driving, keep all car doors locked.
- Never approach alligators, they can outrun a man.

Police assistance:
☎ **911**
from any call box

TELEPHONES

There are telephones in hotel lobbies, drug stores, restaurants, garages and at the roadside. A local call costs 25 cents. Buy cards for long distance calls from the Official Visitors Centre, some pharmacies and grocery stores. Dial '0' for the operator. 'Collect' means reverse the charges.

International Dialling Codes

From Orlando (US) to:

UK:	**011 44**
Ireland:	**011 353**
Australia:	**011 61**
Germany:	**011 49**
Netherlands:	**011 31**
Spain:	**011 34**

POST

Post offices in Orlando are few and far between. Stamps from vending machines are sold at a 25 per cent premium; it is best to buy them at your hotel. The international postcard rate is 80 cents. Post offices are usually open Mon–Fri 9AM–5PM, but many hotels and major attractions provide a post office service out of hours.

ELECTRICITY

The power supply is: 110/120 volts AC (60 cycles)

 Type of socket: sockets take two-prong, flat-pin plugs.

Visitors should bring adaptors for their 3-pin and 2-round-pin plugs.

TIPS/GRATUITIES

Yes ✓   No ✗

It is useful to have plenty of small notes		
Hotels (chambermaid, doorman etc)	✓	$1
Restaurants (waiter, waitresses)	✓	15/20%
Bar Service	✓	15%
Taxis	✓	15%
Tour guides (discretionary)	✓	
Porters	✓	$1 per bag
Hairdressers	✓	15%
Toilets (rest rooms)	✗	

PHOTOGRAPHY

What to photograph: Orlando and its nearby theme parks are great places to take photographs. There are plenty of opportunities for classic Disney shots, as well as those of natural flora and fauna.

When to photograph: The hot summer months can be very humid and may affect photography. The best time of day to photograph is between 1 and 6PM.

Where to buy film: All types of film and photo processing are freely available in drugstores, theme parks etc but it is cheaper to take your own film.

HEALTH

Insurance
Medical insurance cover of at least $1,000,000 unlimited cover is strongly recommended, as medical bills can be astronomical and treatment may be withheld if you have no evidence of means to pay.

Dental Services
Your medical insurance cover should include dental treatment, which is readily available, but expensive. Have a check up before you go. Dental referral telephone numbers are in the Yellow Pages telephone directory or ask at the desk of your hotel.

Sun Advice
By far the most common source of ill health in Florida is too much sun. Orlando in summer is very hot and humid and the sun is strong all year round. Use a sunscreen, wear a hat outdoors and ensure that everyone drinks plenty of fluids.

Drugs
Medicines can be bought at drug stores, certain drugs generally available elsewhere require a prescription in the US. Acetaminophen is the US equivalent of paracetamol. Take an insect repellent including Deet and cover up after dark, to avoid being bitten by mosquitoes.

Safe Water
Restaurants usually provide a jug of iced water. Drinking unboiled water from taps is safe but not always very pleasant. Mineral water is cheap and readily available.

CONCESSIONS

Students/Youths Most concessions at major theme parks apply to children aged 3–9, but some sights and attractions offer special admission prices to bona fide students. There are also concessionary rail fares (International Student Identity Card required as proof).

Senior Citizens (Seniors) Over three million mature travellers visit Orlando each year, in addition to the 'Senior' permanent residents, and many special discounts are available to those over 55. Members of the American Association of Retired Persons, over 50 (AARPs) are eligible (with ID) for discounts on accommodation, meals, car rental, transport and many attractions in the Orlando area.

CLOTHING SIZES

Orlando (USA)	UK	Rest of Europe		
36	36	46		Suits
38	38	48		Suits
40	40	50		Suits
42	42	52		Suits
44	44	54		Suits
46	46	56		Suits
8	7	41		Shoes
8.5	7.5	42		Shoes
9.5	8.5	43		Shoes
10.5	9.5	44		Shoes
11.5	10.5	45		Shoes
12	11	46		Shoes
14.5	14.5	37		Shirts
15	15	38		Shirts
15.5	15.5	39/40		Shirts
16	16	41		Shirts
16.5	16.5	42		Shirts
17	17	43		Shirts
6	8	34		Dresses
8	10	36		Dresses
10	12	38		Dresses
12	14	40		Dresses
14	16	42		Dresses
16	18	44		Dresses
6	4.5	38		Shoes
6.5	5	38		Shoes
7	5.5	39		Shoes
7.5	6	39		Shoes
8	6.5	40		Shoes
8.5	7	41		Shoes

WHEN DEPARTING

- Check airport terminal number (there are three terminals) and allow plenty of time to get there and hand in any rental car.
- Arrive at check-in at least two hours before departure time.
- US Customs are strict. There are no departure taxes but ensure that you have all necessary documentation and that you are not contravening US Customs regulations.

LANGUAGE

The official language of the USA is English, and, given that one third of all overseas visitors come from the UK, Orlando natives have few problems coping with British accents and dialects. Spanish is also widely spoken, as many workers in the hotel and catering industries are of Latin American origin.

Many English words have different meanings and below are some words in common usage where they differ from the English spoken in the UK:

holiday	*vacation*	tap	*faucet*
fortnight	*two weeks*	handbag	*purse*
ground floor	*first floor*	luggage	*baggage*
first floor	*second floor*	suitcase	*trunk*
second floor	*third floor*	hotel porter	*bellhop*
flat	*apartment*	chambermaid	*room maid*
lift	*elevator*	surname	*last name*
eiderdown	*comforter*	cupboard	*closet*

cheque	*check*	25 cent coin	*quarter*
traveller's	*traveler's*	banknote	*bill*
cheque	*check*	banknote (collo-	*greenback*
1 cent coin	*penny*	quial)	
5 cent coin	*nickel*	dollar (colloquial)	*buck*
10 cent coin	*dime*	cashpoint	*automatic teller*

grilled	*broiled*	biscuit	*cookie*
frankfurter	*frank*	scone	*biscuit*
prawns	*shrimp*	sorbet	*sherbet*
aubergine	*eggplant*	jelly	*jello*
courgette	*zucchini*	jam	*jelly*
maize	*corn*	confectionery	*candy*
chips (potato)	*fries*	spirit	*liquor*
crisps (potato)	*chips*	soft drink	*soda*

car	*automobile*	petrol	*gas, gasoline*
bonnet (of car)	*hood*	railway	*railroad*
boot (of car)	*trunk*	tram	*streetcar*
repair	*fix*	underground	*subway*
caravan	*trailer*	platform	*track*
lorry	*truck*	buffer	*bumper*
motorway	*freeway*	single ticket	*one-way ticket*
main road	*highway*	return ticket	*round-trip ticket*

shop	*store*	policeman	*cop*
chemist (shop)	*drugstore*	post	*mail*
cinema	*movie theater*	post code	*zip code*
film	*movie*	ring up,	*call*
pavement	*sidewalk*	telephone	
subway	*underpass*	long-distance	*trunk call*
toilet	*rest room*	call	
trousers	*pants*	autumn	*fall*
nappy	*diaper*	gangway	*aisle*
glasses	*eyeglasses*	car park	*parking lot*

INDEX

Acknowledgements

The Automobile Assocation wishes to thank the following libraries and organisations for their assistance in the preparation of this book:

BUSCH ENTERTAINMENT CORP 27a, 48a, 50; BRUCE COLEMAN COLLECTION 12a; DISCOVERY COVE 18, 30/1, KENNEDY SPACE CENTER 11; KISSIMMEE & ST CLOUD C & VB 9b, 55; LEU GARDENS 13; MARY EVANS PICTURE LIBRARY 10, 14; MRI BANKER'S GUIDE TO FOREIGN CURRENCY 119; P MURPHY 12b, 63; NATURE PHOTOGRAPHERS 61 (P R Sterry); ORLANDO & ORANGE COUNTY C & VB 7a, 34, PICTURES COLOUR LIBRARY 8b, 22; RIPLEY'S BELIEVE IT OR NOT! 35; SPECTRUM COLOUR LIBRARY 16, 27b, 48b, 49; SEA WORLD 15a, 38/9a, 38/9b; UNIVERSAL STUDIOS 26, 41a; THE WALT DISNEY CO. 25, 70, 73, 74/5, 76/7, 78/9, 80, 82/3, 84/5, 87, 89, 90; WET N' WILD 1

The remaining photographs are held in the Association's own library (AA PHOTO LIBRARY) and were taken by Tony Souter, with the exception of the following:
P Bennett 7b, 15b, 20, 21, 47, 60, 62, 66, 117b.
The author would like to thank Jayne Teleska Behrle, Orlando-Orange County Convention and Visitors Bureau, Inc; Hayley Busse, Orlando-Orange County Convention and Visitors Bureau, UK; Larry White, Kissimmee-St Cloud Convention and Visitors Bureau, USA; Sarah Handy, Kissimmee-St Cloud Convention and Visitors Bureau, UK; and Joyce Taylor, Walt Disney Attractions, UK.

This book makes reference to various Disney copyrighted characters, trademarks, marks and registered marks owned by The Walt Disney Company and Disney Enterprises, Inc.

Contributors
Copy editor: Nia Williams   Page Layout: Barfoot Design   Verifier: Paul Murphy
Researcher (Practical Matters): Lesley Allard   Indexer: Marie Lorimer
Revision management: Pam Stagg

Dear Essential Traveller

**Your comments, opinions and recommendations are very
important to us. So please help us to improve our travel
guides by taking a few minutes to complete this simple
questionnaire.**

*You do not need a stamp (unless posted outside the UK). If you do not want to cut this page
from your guide, then photocopy it or write your answers on a plain sheet of paper.*

Send to: **The Editor, AA World Travel Guides,
FREEPOST SCE 4598, Basingstoke RG21 4GY.**

Your recommendations...

We always encourage readers' recommendations for restaurants, nightlife
or shopping – if your recommendation is used in the next edition of the
guide, we will send you a *FREE* AA *Essential* **Guide** of your choice.
Please state below the establishment name, location and your reasons
for recommending it.

_____

_____

_____

_____

Please send me **AA *Essential*** _____
(see list of titles inside the front cover)

About this guide...

Which title did you buy?
    AA *Essential* _____
Where did you buy it? _____
When? __ __ / __ __

Why did you choose an AA *Essential* Guide? _____

_____

_____

_____

_____

Did this guide meet your expectations?
    Exceeded ☐   Met all ☐   Met most ☐   Fell below ☐
    Please give your reasons _____

_____

_____

_____

continued on next page...

Were there any aspects of this guide that you particularly liked? _____
_____
_____
_____

Is there anything we could have done better? _____
_____
_____
_____
_____

About you...

Name (*Mr/Mrs/Ms*) _____
   Address _____
_____
_____ Postcode _____
   Daytime tel nos _____

Which age group are you in?
   Under 25 ☐ 25–34 ☐ 35–44 ☐ 45–54 ☐ 55–64 ☐ 65+ ☐

How many trips do you make a year?
   Less than one ☐ One ☐ Two ☐ Three or more ☐

Are you an AA member? Yes ☐ No ☐

About your trip...

When did you book? m m / y y   When did you travel? m m / y y
How long did you stay? _____
Was it for business or leisure? _____
Did you buy any other travel guides for your trip?
   If yes, which ones? _____
_____

Thank you for taking the time to complete this questionnaire. Please send
   it to us as soon as possible, and remember, you do not need a stamp
   (*unless posted outside the UK*).

Happy Holidays!

Peak HOUR

A Handbook of the Everest Flight

Text by Dubby Bhagat

Research and Photographs by Rik. A.D. Sherpa

Rupa & Co

© Dubby Bhagat and Rik.A.D. Sherpa 1994

An Original Rupa Paperback

First published 1994 by
Rupa & Co
7/16 Ansari Road, Daryaganj, New Delhi 110 002
15 Bankim Chatterjee Street, Calcutta 700 073
135 South Malaka, Allahabad 211 001
P.G. Solanki Path, Lamington Road, Bombay 400 007

Peak Hour is designed, illustrated and typeset by
Arrt Creations
45 Nehru Apartments
Kalkajee, New Delhi-110 019.

Typeset in Palatino 14 pt.

Printed by
Gopsons Papers Pvt Ltd
A-28 Sector IX
Noida 201 301

Rs. 295

ISBN   81 - 7167 - 206 - X

To Nina
with love
from Dolly & Mohini
22nd Aug 84

For my mother, Mohini Bhagat, who taught me about myths and once laboured up a mountain with me.

For R. K. Mehra, publisher and friend, whose idea this is.

For Lari Sahib and Mrs. Najma Lari who have put up with me and supported me for over a decade. These words are in lieu of the medal they so richly deserve.

CONTENTS

AUTHOR'S NOTE

I have deliberately used the word 'Himalaya' as it is closer to the Sanskrit etymology of the name. However, in reporting other people's speech, I have used the popular name — Himalayas.

ACKNOWLEDGEMENTS

We hover, Rik. A.D. Sherpa and I, in that uncertain area between gratitude and guilt. We are grateful, endlessly so, for all the help we got and vaguely guilty because we suspect we cannot ever repay the debt.

So in writing it all down here we move a little, just a little, away from the old guilt towards healthy gratitude.

Utpal and Caroline Sengupta came forward with a do-it-yourself writer's kit that ranged from pens to paper clips. And there was always encouragement when it was needed. And food. And friendship.

Vish and Anjeli Sowani actually funded an expedition into the Khumbu. Complete with a camera, film, guides, porters. Butter lamps were lit for them in Thyangboche monastery as inadequate thanks.

Brian Whyte not only gave a vastness of hospitality at his 'Brigand's Bend', where this book was conceived, he also edited all that follows and in so doing all but wrote the book.

Liz Hawley, the ultimate Himalayan expert who knows more about the mountains than mountaineers, gave freely of her time. And though her patience must have worn thin with the questioning, she never threw anything at us.

Jug and Bunny Suraiya who live in distant Delhi gave the book a title that defined and directed it. Bunny even edited this in its final stages in expectation of a vastness of chewing gum which she eventually went and bought herself.

Lisa Choegyal and Stan Armington gave tomes and volumes to browse through and answered absolutely inane questions about the mountains they know so well.

Muni and Sheila Rana and Mike Malinovski made writing possible with special paper to write on. Without them, literally, the book would never have been written.

Shekhar Lama took the manuscript from untidy scrawl to computer perfect via a typewriter. In doing so, he did the impossible: read my handwriting.

Willy Gurung lent the typewriter and the courage to write.

D. N. Lohani, Nepal's most famous astrologer, told stories of the gods and the planets and gave the exact time to start the book, finish it and hand it in.

Nepal Airways and Necon Air took us on mountain flights and into the mountains. They did so without charging us. Wonderful people.

Prasad Moktan and the Lotus Studio gang did the pictures for us in double quick time.

In Delhi, Kiran Sant and his Exotic Tours and Deepika Metha provided unrepayable back-up.

And all at World Travels Nepal helped in ways too numerous to count.

Himalayan thanks to all of you. You are owed a lot.

FOREWORD

Everest from Kala Pathar.

HIMALAYAN TRUST

Chairman :
Sir Edmund Hillary,
278A Remuera Road,
Auckland 5, New Zealand.
Telephone: 520-3169
Fax: 64-9-520-7847

22nd December, 1993

"There are probably few people who have a wider knowledge of the culture, religion and mythology of Nepal than Dubby Bhagat. To travel with him around the ancient shrines of Kathmandu is an experience in itself. Although not claiming to be a mountaineer he has accumulated a vast body of wisdom on the great peaks of the Himalayas and their peoples and mythology. This is not a book for those who want to be guided to the summit of Mt. Everest. But if you want a fascinating romantic story of Nepal and its great mountains you will undoubtedly find it in Dubby Bhagat's narrative."

Sir Edmund Hillary

MOUNTAINS OF THE EVEREST FLIGHT

TRIPPING THE
FLIGHT FANTASTIC

et's strip it down to its bare essentials.

On the mountain flight you will see twenty-one mountains.

Six of them are over 8000 metres high.

Seven of them are over 7000 metres high.

Seven of them are over 6000 metres high.

Only one is a 5000-metre mountain and it hasn't been climbed.

You will see Everest which is the highest mountain in the world.

You are traversing the Eastern Nepal Himalaya, the 'rising sun range', which comprises some of the earth's loftiest summits.

These pages will give you something of the myths, miracles and magic these mountains are steeped in. They will tell you of the people who inhabit the mountains, the people who discovered them and the people who climbed them.

Each of the mountains you pass has a mythical and chronological past and as a group, these Himalaya are filled with enchantment.

We are going to meet sages on flying white tigers,

sorcerers, gods, goddesses, magicians whose source of power lies in the mountains. Lakes that wash away sin. Peaks that are celestial abodes. Monasteries that are prayers to the mountains. Hidden secret valleys where no one ages. You will meet knights, kings, queens, adventurers, a dragon, several demons ....

All these are the stuff of mountains.

And you will have the beginnings of understanding the Himalaya. Just glimmerings. No one flight or one book can tell it all. You will understand this as you go gently past them.

Think of it: you are seeing 65 million years of evolution and a billion dreams of Man. Your own dream will add to the awe of the Himalaya and the mountains will give you a vision that will live with you, travel with you and nurture you wherever you are, whatever you do.

This is the promise of the Himalaya and of the mountain flight.

Guru Padma Sambhava in Lukla Monastery.

WHERE MYTHS
AND
MOUNTAINS MEET

The Keeper of Secrets, regal in his ochre and burgundy robes, turned the pages of an ancient manuscript and said, "Tell those who wish to view our mountains that they are as young as yesterday and as old as the times when the gods walked this earth.

"Tell them of the great ocean from which the mountains were born, an ocean that gave birth to the gods themselves.

"That ocean was filled, first with gold, then with silver, then with precious stones. And when the ocean was no more, then the gods made the mountains.

"They used the mud, the rocks, the very stuff of oceans. They used granite and stone.

"And when they were content, the gods blew cold winds onto their creation. And snow and ice formed and lived on the mountains ever since.

"We Sherpas, and the Tibetans from whom we are descended, called these mountains Kang Ri, 'Snow Mountain'.

"But we were given that name from the Sanskrit language of India where they were known as Himalaya, 'Abode of the Snows'."

Amazingly, religion and geography touch several times

when it comes to the creation of the Himalaya.

There was indeed a vast ocean. Known as the Sea of Tethys, it separated India from Eurasia. Then 65 million years ago India started drifting towards Eurasia.

65 million years ago, the two land masses crashed under the sea. Upheaval. And the Himalaya was born.

They are the youngest and highest mountains in the world and are still growing because the unrelenting Indian continent continues to move northward at the speed of 2 to 5 cm a year, pushing peaks even higher.

But if you're not satisfied with a vast ocean simply disappearing merely because two land masses collide, turn to one of Hinduism's most poignant tales.

In the beginning Vishnu, the Preserver of Life, was on the shore of a vast sea. His only companions were a pair of seagulls. Every now and then the female seagull would lay eggs only to have the sea wash them away. So she'd build her nest and lay her eggs farther and farther away but the malevolent sea would follow her and wash them away.

In despair, the gulls appealed to Vishnu. And the Preserver of Life opened his mouth and swallowed the sea. It was as if the waters never were and there, instead, was Mother Earth.

The Keeper of Secrets, The Reincarnate Lama of
Thyangboche Monastery, Ngwang Tenzing Zangbu.

The oceanic origins of the Himalaya still remain in Ammonites or Saligram — sea things found 400 metres up in the mountains.

Beautifully shaped, as big as shells, these Saligrams — as Sanskrit knows them — are an essential part of religious tradition.

On a far grander scale, the Nuptse-Lhotse wall that screens Everest has huge bands of sedimentary rocks typically seen on ocean floors.

There is too, as proof positive, the race memory of Himalayan people and their love of corals. How else, it is argued, could mountain people love oceanic objects were it not for faint echoes of the vanished Sea of Tethys?

And they remember Tethys in the Greek classics too. It is the sea from whose foam Aphrodite was created. Of that age she still remains.

And the Himalaya.

Sir George Everest.

MAPPING MOUNTAINS

"I n a hundred ages of the Gods I could not tell thee of the glories of the Himalaya.

As the dew is dried by the morning sun, so are the sins of man by the sight of the Himalaya."

That exquisite little saying is taken from the *Skanda Purana*, an ancient Hindu text.

And there are entire libraries full of exquisite, wise, clever sayings about the Himalaya. The whole Indian subcontinent gazed at those magnificent mountains for thousands of years, writing about them, worshipping them, and going on pilgrimage amongst them.

But no one really did anything practical about them.

Then in 1597, when the Moghul Emperor Akbar ruled Hindustan, the Spanish Jesuit, Father Anthony Montserrat, came to his court.

A few years later Father Montserrat drew a map that bore a resemblance to the Himalaya.

After that the Himalaya became a hive of exploring activity. There was the Frenchman — Jean Baptiste d'Anville — who produced an *Atlas of China* and another map called *Carte de l'Inde* in the 18th century.

A little later, Captain James Renell, who had become the first Surveyor-General of Bengal, went into retirement and produced his *Map of Hindoostan* which was newer and better than d'Anville's map but which copied d'Anville when it came to, amongst other parts of the chain, the Nepal Himalaya.

Slowly the Nepal Himalaya was shaped on maps by a succession of journeyers including Johann Gruber and Albert d'Orville who were the first Europeans to get to Lhasa and who travelled from there to Kathmandu and Agra. Both were missionaries.

By the turn of the 19th century, a British Resident was installed in Kathmandu and the commander of the escort was one Charles Crawford who hinted at the great heights of the Himalaya.

Then in 1809, Lieutenant W.S. Webb, who was exploring the upper reaches of the River Ganges in the Kumaun Himalaya, calculated that a mountain in neighbouring Nepal was over 8000 metres high. It was called Dhaulagiri.

Now think of this. The year is 1809. The world is introduced to a peak a shade over 8000 metres high. Does it applaud Webb? Does it decorate Webb? No. It ridicules Webb. For the oldest reason in the world: the experts know better.

Because until 1809, geographers the world over were convinced that Chimborazo, in the Andes, was the highest mountain in the world.

Just 40 years later, while working in Bihar in the Gangetic plain of India, surveyors discovered a peak even higher than Dhaulagiri. It was called 'Peak XV' and upon recomputation in 1852, this numerically named peak was declared the highest in the world. It too was in Nepal.

Nepal! Nepal! Nepal! Here was a country that had a cache of high mountains. Here was a place that was waiting to be explored, mapped, measured; but the British in India couldn't get to it. Nepal was forbidden. Nepal, with its jungle beginnings that abutted India, was protected by a mysterious and lethal disease called 'awl'. If one caught it, high fevers, delirium and death followed. It was malaria, of course, but that was discovered later.

So throughout the 19th century, vague reports of peaks that seemingly touched the sky, of a strange religion called Mahayana Buddhism that one British Resident in Kathmandu wrote about, and of a kindly but courageous people, filtered out to the world, tantalising it but never being confirmed.

That strange and arcane body, the Great Trigonometrical Survey of India, had to be content with mapping around Nepal, which they did with great efficiency.

The British India Survey continued its work into the 20th
century. The picture, taken in 1904, shows officials
taking zenith observations : the British officer at the
telescope is observing a star, calling out readings which
are noted by his assistant at the table.
The observations helped fill in the map of the Great
Trigonometrical Survey of India.

One of the heads of the Great Trigonometrical Survey was George Everest who found new and accurate ways of measuring the heights of mountains. He retired in 1843 and it was Andrew Waugh, his successor, who suggested that 'Peak XV' be renamed Everest. The name stuck. Everest himself enjoyed the knowledge that the world's highest mountain carried his name for a scant year before he died, in 1866.

As Nepal was closed to Europeans, except of course the British Residents who were reluctantly allowed to stay, it fell upon fourteen Indian topographers between 1924 and 1927 to detail the lowlands of the country right up to the foothills of the Himalaya.

It was only in 1950 after Nepal opened its doors, that the Research Scheme Nepal Himalaya led by E. Schneider actually drew definitive maps of the Nepal Himalaya. They are used to this day.

Think of it. What was begun in 1579 was completed only in the 1950s. The mapping of a continent. The investigation of a unique part of the world. The revelation of one of the last secrets.

Kipling, that poet of the Empire, wrote:

'Something hidden. Go and find it.

Go and look behind the Ranges —

Khapa Gyaltzen and his wife. He is an artist of mountains in Sherpa style. Khapa means artist.

A Meyul or Beyul by Ghaltzen the Sherpa artist.

Something lost behind the Ranges.

Lost and waiting for you. Go.'

He summed up the western attitude to the mountains. Explore them. Don't leave a secret unturned.

The eastern view was one of romance and philosophy. It was a state of mind that said: 'Aren't they tall, wondrous, beautiful? Let's leave them for sunrises, sunsets, odes and contemplation.'

One wonders which attitude is right. And then one wonders if being right has anything to do with life or with what actually happens.

A Mani or Prayer Wall high up in Sherpa country.

SECRETS,
SANCTUARIES
AND SHERPAS

The Keeper of Secrets was silent as gongs, cymbals and horns sounded an end to the soft murmur of the evening prayers. "Our name 'Sherpa' means 'Man from the East'. We came six hundred years ago from Kham in eastern Tibet."

"We settled in the high and lonely places in the mountains."

"They were sacred, these places, and our religious books refer to them as 'Beyul' or 'Meyul'. The words mean sanctuary."

"We found and settled most of these secret, sacred places. Except one."

"Khanbalung is a hidden valley where people will age slowly. It has not yet been opened to all. Khanbalung sits at the centre of a ring of hidden valleys...."

Could James Hilton have known of Khanbalung, of 'Beyuls' and 'Meyuls'? He called his sanctuary 'Shangrila' and his Keeper of Secrets was a High Lama. And his book, *Lost Horizon*, has a European stumbling into an enchanted place surrounded by mountains, where people age slowly and are infinitely wise.

Khanbalung must be well hidden indeed. The Sherpas who inhabit highland Nepal have not found it yet. A happy, hospitable, rambunctious people, the Sherpas, who are traders and farmers, would have invited the world into their Shangrila — for a price.

When you fly the mountains, think of these people who inhabit them, who have given them names and whose gods live on top of some of the peaks you pass.

The Sherpas have helped the world in its quest for summits, first as high altitude porters and more recently as skilled climbers.

For convenience, I divide the Sherpas into four groups who live in different parts of the Himalaya.

The Sherpas of the Khumbu area around Everest consider themselves closest to their Tibetan origins and, until recently, kept in touch with Tibet through the salt routes.

The Solu Sherpas are cannier, have larger plots of land, and though the language they speak is almost the same as that of Khumbu Sherpas, they speak it slowly.

For most Solu Sherpas, communication for trade has resulted in Nepali becoming a first language and Sherpali being virtually forgotten.

They live in the shadows of mountains like Numbur.

The Helambu Sherpas, near Langtang Lirung, speak a dialect that neither the Solu nor Khumbu Sherpas understand. Of late, the Helambu Sherpas have started

Thyangboche Monastery.

Thyangboche Monastery by
Khapa Gyaltzen, the Sherpa artist.

Prayer Wheel at Lukla Monastery.

venturing out to India as contractors, traders and, often, as settlers.

The Sherpas who live near Kanchenjunga are adopting Sanskrit names. And whereas they understand Sherpali they are beginning to forget how to speak it. Slowly these Sherpas are adopting Hindu customs.

For the most part, Sherpas follow either Mahayana or Vajrayana schools of Buddhism, getting other people to kill animals for them to eat. Or better still, driving yaks off high cliffs so that the fall does the killing.

Because of their long history as traders, the Sherpas have a chameleon-like quality of being able to mingle easily with\other races, other communities. Westerners love Sherpas and have encouraged their participation in the growing tourism industry of Nepal.

It's strange to see a Sherpa whizz around Kathmandu in a car or on a bike when you consider the fact that the only wheels in their remote high world are the constantly turning prayer wheels that invoke the many names of the Compassionate Buddha.

Lho La, Everest and Nuptse from Kala Pathar.

GOING TO MEET
THE MOUNTAINS

When I was in school, my Geography teacher, who was just a few years older than I, taught me about mountains.

He loved the mountains and while dissecting them for his students to understand them better, he performed an amazing act: he imbued these still and lofty giants with human qualities that made them real for us.

He talked of the mountains with passion and feeling and some of it must have rubbed off because I longed to be amongst them.

So I went on treks in the Garhwal Himalaya.

For me, this was quite an achievement and an even bigger one for Hari Dang, my Geography teacher. You see, I hate the outdoors and I hate all forms of exercise and still do. My late father predicted that I would be 'bone idle'. How right he was.

My natural habitat is rooms. Preferably smoke-and conversation-filled. But Hari Dang had instilled a love of mountains in me. How to reconcile the two?

I was lucky. It was given to me to meet mountaineers and to settle down and work in Kathmandu from where the mountains were visible even from smoke - and conversation - filled interiors.

The first mountaineer I ever met was Hari Dang, though

Sir Edmund Hillary.

Desmond Doig.

neither of us knew it at the time. In his living room he had a picture of the Annapurna Sanctuary which he idealised as a place of great peace away from noisesome adolescents.

On a recent trip to Kathmandu, he paused in a busy schedule to meet me.

"Did you ever climb Annapurna?" I asked.

"No," he said. "But I tried for the Big One. And missed."

Hari Dang was on the 1962 Indian Everest Expedition and was forced back along with the peak assault team at 8720 metres, just 128 metres away from the summit.

But in a sense Hari Dang made it to the top in 1965 when a summiteer, Sonam Gyatso, placed a Hindu rosary belonging to Hari Dang on the peak of Mt. Everest.

In the hurly-burly of my life the mountains receded to the back of my mind where they were a symbol of things to be achieved and then much, much later I met Desmond Doig. He was my editor when I worked for the *Junior Statesman*, and through our years together until he died in 1983, he was my mentor, teacher and friend.

Desmond Doig was not so much a mountaineer as a scribe to expeditions. He went into the mountains with Sir Edmund Hillary and a host of luminaries to hunt for the Yeti, to winter at high altitudes and to record the ascent of Makalu.

He wrote a book with Sir Edmund called *High in the Thin Cold Air* and there was a time when a Desmond Doig article in *The National Geographic* meant a detailed look into things Himalayan — Nepal, Bhutan, Sikkim. Desmond loved all these mountain kingdoms and wrote about them with such texture that readers the world over were drawn to them.

It was through Desmond Doig that I met Sir Edmund Hillary first in Calcutta and afterwards in Kathmandu.

Ed, as he likes to be called, is as rugged as the mountains he climbs but never as lofty. He covers an abiding modesty and kindness with a gruff exterior.

After he became the first man to climb Mount Everest, Ed spent his time bringing schools and hospitals into his beloved Khumbu, the area around Everest. And many are the Sherpa doctors, rangers and climbers who owe their success to a Hillary school.

I once met Ed as he came back to Kathmandu and told him of the success of the most recent Everest expedition. "Ah yes," Ed said, "I read about it. They took the tourist route up." What Ed describes so modestly as 'the tourist route', is the one he and Tenzing Norgay pioneered in 1953.

Another time, when I was Director of Sales and Marketing at the Everest Hotel in Kathmandu — a property which I am still attached and addicted to — I asked Ed to help me launch a drink which would be called the Hillary Conquest. Ed really didn't have to do it but he took the time between meetings, lectures and receptions to sit down at the bar of the Everest, sample five drinks and choose one.

The Hillary Conquest is a best-selling cocktail at the Everest Hotel. Even in passing, Sir Edmund has a surefire touch.

It was Ed who brought Mike Gill into my life and of Mike Gill it was said, always behind his back, that if he hadn't become a mountaineer, he would have made a fine cat burglar. He skims up seemingly impossible surfaces and Ama Dablam and Kangtega have, amongst others, succumbed to his skills.

I first met Mike at Desmond Doig's Calcutta flat. He was on his way up the Ganges in speedboats with Edmund Hillary in an adventure that Ed chronicled in *From the Ocean to the Sky*.

I was broke at the time and about to get married. Very unobtrusively, Mike became the wedding photographer. The marriage didn't last. The photographs did. And both my ex-wife and I have the fondest memories of

Jimmy Roberts, Mountaineer and
Trekking Pioneer. Photograph courtesy:
Tiger Mountain Archives.

Mike Gill.

I came up to Kathmandu in 1965. The city was peopled with mountaineers. Some had climbed mountains, some were about to climb mountains and some dreamed of impossible mountains and extravagant expeditions. One of the most practical mountaineers I met was Colonel Jimmy Roberts just after he'd been co-leader on the 1971 International Everest Expedition. He'd started trekking in Nepal in 1964 and was immensely success-ful. Over the years, Jimmy dropped both mountaineer-ing and trekking and went to live in Pokhara, the little valley town named for its famous lake which reflects spectacular views of the Himalaya.

Jimmy raises pheasants at his home in Pokhara and on one occasion when I visited him there, he said that the birds were less demanding than people.

I knew what he meant. He had more time to himself with his pheasants than he ever had in his always-crowded trekking office in Kathmandu.

Out of his window in Pokhara, Jimmy can look out and see Machhapuchchhare, a beautiful, unclimbed, forbid-den peak. It must come as a relief to Jimmy that there are some spots still sacred to human beings. Some say that Jimmy actually campaigned to declare the peak off-limits to climbers. I've never got around to asking him if the rumour was true.

Another mountaineer who turned trekker and sends hundreds of people into the mountains every year is Stan Armington. Stan gave up mountaineering because, "I was fed up of being cold and I didn't want to die!"

One of the people he took trekking was President Jimmy Carter.

After his trek, Carter was so pleased with Stan's arrangements that he asked Stan if there was anything he could do for him in the States.

Stan told President Carter that his years in Nepal had kept him from being an ideal son and he would be grateful if President Carter would ring up his father at home in the United States.

Armington Senior was in hospital when the President rang and a flustered nurse rushed the phone to his bedside, saying: "You'll never guess who this is!" "Ronald Reagan?" asked Stan's father.

"My goodness, you know him too!" the nurse exclaimed, handing over the phone.

Recently Stan was compelled by my sheer persistence to give me a copy of his best-selling Lonely Planet Guide to *Trekking in the Nepal Himalaya*. In his inscription he remembered our, literally, thousands of dinners together. At each meal I learned a little more about the mountains, about the people who live amongst them and the people who climb them. A few more dinners and I'll be an authority. I'm a slow learner and Stan is a MENSA certified genius.

It was Stan Armington who pointed out Reinhold Messner to me in the busy streets of Kathmandu. Reinhold Messner whom the mountaineering world considers today's greatest technical climber, has climbed all 14 of the 8000-metre peaks and is considered one of the best mountaineers of our time.

I met Messner every day for days on end when he stayed at the Everest Hotel and I was asked to look after him. What struck me most about him was his beatific grin. He didn't demand anything special and went about preparing for his Cho-Oyu climb with a matter-of-factness that you and I assume while going to work.

He was going to work. But his work was climbing mountains where, according to him, chances of survival hovered around 50% and he was doing it for the charge of adrenalin that gives mountaineers an addictive high. He talked about this — not to me, but in my hearing — as I hovered about seeing that his stay in the Everest Hotel was all it should be.

I don't claim to know Messner beyond the mandatory

Reinhold Messner

handshake and the exchange of pleasantries that take place between a V.I.P. guest and a hotel employee. But one thing did strike me about him. Messner, despite his entourage, was a reclusive kind of person who had achieved a degree of comfort within himself.

I am not surprised that it was he who made the first solo ascent of Everest. He struck me as the kind of person who would actually enjoy not just the challenge of the mountain but the joy of being alone on it.

Whenever I think of Messner, I think of that extraordinary smile of a person who has experienced danger, faced death and has come to terms with them. And also with this business of living.

If Messner is one extreme of mountaineering then Barry Bishop is the convivial other extreme. It was Desmond Doig who introduced me to Barry Bishop and his charming wife, Laila. Barry climbed Everest and, with Mike Gill, was on the first ascent of Ama Dablam.

He'd worked in Nepal for a long time, preparing for a doctorate on a remote mountainous area. He now works for *The National Geographic* and has promoted so much talent that he deserves the ultimate accolade — that of being a universal patron. Of writing, of art, of science. But Barry wears it all well. For me he is a sort of Salvador Dali of the mountains. Quirky, independent, a free spirit.

There was a time when a young photographer came to Desmond Doig's house in Kathmandu with an impressive portfolio of pictures. Desmond sent him to Barry Bishop in America. And the world, through Barry and *The National Geographic*, discovered the work of Eric Valli.

When Bradford Washburn, the eminent cartographer, was photographing and making a new map of the Everest region, it was Barry who stepped in when the going got rough. And it is Barry and Laila who make their home your casa if you happen to be in America and you happen to be from Nepal.

I phoned Barry at *The National Geographic* when I was in New York. He'd just got a promotion. While I congratulated him, I expressed fear that his new, elevated position wouldn't allow him time enough to visit Nepal.

It was typical of Barry to say, "That position hasn't been invented yet."

Barry Bishop is positively gregarious when compared to the only Japanese mountaineer I know — Takashi Ozaki, who has been up six 8000-metre peaks seven times. He is one of the few mountaineers who puts up with my naïve and incredibly stupid questions. And

Takashi has the knack of answering them in such a considered manner that I do not feel naïve and incredibly stupid.

I once asked him if he wasn't worried about surprising or startling a god on the mountains he climbed. "That is an old belief," said Takashi, "I don't think the gods live on mountains any more."

I think Takashi stopped climbing once Messner had climbed all the 8000-metre peaks. Despite the fact that Takashi admires Messner, I feel Takashi thought that there was nothing left to do.

Besides, Takashi has responsibilities now: his wonderful French wife, Frederique, and their children, Makoto and Sarah. And even as I sit writing this in Nepal, Takashi is writing a book in Japan. The world might well have lost a famous mountaineer but it's going to gain some truly great books when Takashi comes out in print.

Even as this is written there are commemorative postage stamps being issued in Nepal with the late Sungdare Sherpa on them. I never met Sungdare Sherpa but he was the friend of my co-author, Rik. A.D. Sherpa. The two went on a Dhaulagiri expedition together and A.D. thought Sungdare was a simple person, gifted with the ability of climbing anything, anytime.

Sungdare climbed Everest on five occasions and he took

Takashi Ozaki by Frederique Gely Ozaki.

a bottle or two along each time. Sungdare loved his tipple. A.D. said he once asked Sungdare why he drank so much and Sungdare replied, "What drink? This is my petrol."

In Sherpa circles, there is a story about Sungdare that typifies him. After his fifth ascent of Everest, a certain very high personage asked the Sherpa to name anything in the world and it would be his.

Sungdare thought for a moment and said, "May I please stop being a high-altitude Sherpa and become a high-altitude Leader? The pay is better."

Sungdare didn't die on a mountain. He died in an accident on the way home from a party. The whole of Nepal mourned his passing. And Sherpas still light butter lamps in his memory.

In the eighth century, there was a Chinese poet, Li Po, who beautifully expressed what every mountaineer must feel:

"Up high all the birds have flown away,
A single cloud drifts across the sky.
We settle down together, never tiring of each other,
Only the two of us, the mountain and I."

Li Po climbed Tai Shan in China and used to spend his time with hermits in mountains.

He thought of himself as an immortal who was

Sungdare Sherpa

The Himalaya and Marigolds.
Artist Animesh Roy's interpretation of
the mountains.

Desmond Doig, Dawa Tenzing and Stan Armington.

banished from heaven and was doomed to seek his immortality, never quite finding it, but achieving near salvation in the mountains.

"Why, you ask, do I live up these blue mountains?
I smile and do not reply. Leave me in peace...
There is another sky, another earth, beyond the world of men."

On the seventh floor of the Everest Hotel, arguably the highest point in the valley, I helped to create a restaurant called Sherpaland. Here you can eat Momo and Kothay and other Tibeto-Sherpa delicacies.

But that is not why I planned Sherpaland.

It was designed so that while eating you can see 180 Himalayan peaks. You'll find me there of an afternoon in winter when the mountains are white against clear skies. I'm the portly, lazy, full-of-food chap whose gaze is intense enough to melt the snows.

But what I'm thinking while I take in all the peaks, is of a time when the owners of the airlines that do mountain flights will come up to me and say, "Dubby, here's a season ticket. You can fly the Himalaya every day." And I would fly every day. After all, many of you travel daily to worship, don't you?

LANGTANG
LIRUNG

23,510 feet/7,234 metres

You can see the upper bit of Langtang Lirung from Kathmandu Valley, but getting there is a problem.

First you've got to find Langtang which is one of those hidden 'beyuls' or 'meyuls' or sanctuaries concealed by the gods of Buddhism.

So you travel to Tarke Ghyang, the biggest village in the Helambu region roughly north of Kathmandu. It's a fascinating place, known for its beautiful women, its small, sweet apples and the magical monk of Tarke Ghyang village.

In the early quarter of the 18th century, a terrible plague struck Kathmandu and the king sent for the Magical Monk. The plague was stopped and as reward the monk asked for 100 horses which he took back to Helambu. Around the monk and his horses a village sprang and a gompa, a Buddhist shrine. It was called Tarke Ghyang, or the 'Shrine of 100 Horses'.

The village of Tarke Ghyang is still there and so is the strangely Bhutanese-looking shrine. A faintly ribald Nepali refrain is sung about the shrine which says.

"Tarke Ghyang's shrine,
Now listen all of you,
Has phalluses at each corner
Now listen all of you."

The protective phalluses are common in Bhutan but worth singing about in Nepal.

It was from Tarke Ghyang, or so I like to believe, that long, long ago, a Yak strayed and got lost. But it was a considerate Yak and it left its hoof prints on rocks as it went. Its keeper, coincidentally a monk, followed its trail, crossed a ridge a few days later and stumbled into a beautiful valley — the Langtang Valley.

By the time the monk got there the Yak was dead. So the monk skinned the Yak and laid the hide out to dry. It petrified, and at Langsisa, in the valley, is a red rock that everyone says is the Yak's skin.

So Langtang means 'to follow the yak'.

From here the Lirung. It's a sharp peak when seen from the west and means 'vertical'.

In 1949 Harold William Tillman, explorer, climber and writer, saw Langtang Lirung and wanted to climb it but did not. His book, *Nepal Himalaya,* published in 1952, talks about the mountain. He was the first European in the area.

Between Tillman's time and the early 70s, someone solo-climbed Langtang Lirung unofficially.

The peak was put on the permitted list in 1978.

And it was in the autumn of 1978 that a Japanese-Nepali

Langtang Lirung from a Necon Air flight.

team climbed Langtang Lirung. Seishi Wada and Pemba Tshering Sherpa went up the East Ridge on October, 24.

But despite their success, a persistent rumour of danger shrouds Langtang Lirung and avalanches have had people disappearing. As many as 15 have died in attempts to ascend the Lirung.

From the air and from Kathmandu, Langtang Lirung loses its menace and appears, simply, spectacular.

GOSAINTHAN/ SHISHA PANGMA

26,042 feet/8,013 metres

ven the name is elusive.

The mountain lies a few miles into Tibet and should be called what the Tibetans and Sherpas want it to be called, which is Shisha Pangma. Besides, it has been mapped and climbed as Shisha Pangma.

But the Hindus of Nepal insist on calling it Gosainthan. And now the Chinese tell us it is actually Xixabangma which is pronounced Shisha Pangma but spelled differently.

Assuming that mountains, like roses by any name, are basically the same, let's delve into their nomenclature.

Shisha could mean 'comb' in Sherpa or Tibetan, and Pangma means 'flat place'. So the mountain is the 'Comb that Rises from a Flat Place'. And from certain angles, with its serrated ice, the mountain does look like a fancy comb.

But Shisha is also a well-accepted Hindi word for 'glass' or 'mirror'; so it could also mean the 'Glass or Mirror that Rises from a Flat Place'. And indeed, when the sun is high, Shisha Pangma glistens.

You choose the meaning you like.

Because of the mystery and mythology and romance attached to it, Gosainthan, as a name, has a resonance of timelessness.

The Himalaya are associated with the Hindu God Shiva. His wife Parvati — from whom the word 'Parbat' or peak is derived — was the daughter of a Hindu deity called Himalaya whose legendary palace in the snows has poems in ancient Sanskrit written about it.

Shiva is the Destroyer in the Hindu Trinity but has many aspects, or disguises, to make himself more accessible to simple folk.

One of these is that of the ascetic, meditating in the mountains. In this aspect, while he was once meditating, the other gods decided to churn the oceans looking for the Nectar of Immortality. They used a mountain called Mandara as a churning stick. As they churned, butter was discovered, and the horse of the Sun, and a wish-fulfilling tree.

And as they churned, Poison emerged from the sea.

Shiva rose from his meditation, sensing danger for the other gods. He drank the poison and saved them. But ravaged by pain and thirst, his throat tinged blue by the poison, Shiva thrust his trident or 'trishul' into a mountainside. Three clear springs of water spouted out and collected in a hollow beneath. And Gosainkund Lake was born.

There is to this day a rock at the centre of Gosainkund Lake that believers say is a Shiva manifestation. And once a year on the full moon between mid-July and mid-August, thousands of pilgrims come to Gosainkund to worship Shiva.

Gosainkund is a place of particular pilgrimage.

Gosainthan is a mere 18 kilometres from Gosainkund Lake.

Gosainthan means 'Abode of the God' or 'Place of the Saint'.

Shiva, it is believed, lives atop Mount Kailash in Tibet. Could Gosainthan then be the place where he meditated? Could Gosainthan be the mountain the gods used as a churn? Or is Gosainthan blessed because it is closest to Gosainkund Lake?

Whatever the answer, until recently the Nepalis drew their national border to include the summit so that believers could rightfully climb to the top of Gosainthan. No one in Nepal ever doubted that a believer could climb an 8013-metre peak. But the mountain was — and is — certainly in Tibet.

Just to see Gosainthan or Shisha Pangma has always been a problem.

A 1921 British Mount Everest Expedition, while descending from the Tang La in Tibet, caught sight of Gosainthan to the west.

Heinreich Harrer and Peter Aufschnaiter, who escaped from a British POW Camp in Dehra Dun in India and whose experiences are detailed in the book *Seven Years in Tibet,* actually sketched a panorama of Gosainthan and other mountains in November 1945.

Tillman saw the mountain briefly in 1949 some 20 km away from a glacier on the Lirung. After one glimpse, Gosainthan swirled away into the mists.

In 1950, Toni Hagen, a famous geologist and authority on Nepal, flew over Gosainthan and photographed it.

In 1952, he walked into the area and photographed it again.

Finally in a pre-expedition reconnaissance in 1963, the Chinese got to 7160 metres on the northern slope of Gosainthan or Shisha Pangma.

And in 1964 an expedition of 195 Chinese, headed by Hsu Ching, descended on Gosainthan-Shisha Pangma. On May 2, ten members reached the summit.

It was the last over-8000-metre peak to be ascended.

A lady climber, Japanese housewife and lecturer Junko Tabei, climbed Gosainthan-Shisha Pangma in 1981; Messner in 1982, Jerzy Kukuczka, the famous Polish climber, got to the top in 1987 and Noburo Yamada of Japan in 1988.

Gosainthan by Frederique Gely Ozaki.

Takashi Ozaki who climbed Gosainthan-Shisha Pangma in 1986 had an extraordinary mystical experience as he ventured to the summit.

He kept seeing the face of his newborn son, Makoto. The child didn't say anything. He was merely present.

And Takashi Ozaki, who had climbed Everest twice and who had climbed several other 8000-metre peaks, never climbed a mountain again.

There is a romanticism in me that has me view the mountain as an entity that imbues those who would climb it with the spirit of a pilgrim. And in a sense all mountaineers are pilgrims in a quest for the unreachable. But surely Gosainthan, possessed of the presence of Shiva, would demand an extra spiritual tithe from those who would dare climb it.

For they who have sinned, a bath in the chill waters of Gosainkund Lake is one way of purification. In Kathmandu, near a five-tiered pagoda temple, called Khumbeshwar, is a spring and it is said that its waters come from Gosainkund. To bathe in this pool, too, is to gain absolution.

I like to think that contemplating and wishing upon Gosainthan has the same merit as climbing it, for surely Shiva understands the feebleness of Man.

Shiva as an ascetic.

DORJE LAKPA

22,668 feet/6,975 metres

"Isn't that the peak that was named after the Sherpa who helped an expedition to climb it?" asked a friend. Dorje Lakpa is not a common Sherpa name whereas Lakpa Dorje is.

Sherpas are named after the day of their birth. So Nima is Sunday's child. While a Dawa and a Dorje are born on a Monday. Tuesday is for Mingma. Wednesday's children are Lakpas and the Thursday-born get the name Phurba. Fridays are for Pasangs and Saturdays, Pembas.

It's easy to tell on which day a Sherpa was born, but it's much more difficult to tell the month or the year.

Besides being a name, Dorje also means 'sacred thunderbolt', and many Dorjes are said to have fallen from the heavens onto earth. The Holy Swayambhunath Temple in Kathmandu Valley is on a hill that is said to be one such Dorje or sacred thunderbolt that fell from the heavens.

Lakpa means 'many' or 'much'.

Dorje Lakpa, the Sherpas say, is a mountain of 'Many Sacred Thunderbolts'. A thunderbolt, as interpreted by Buddhism, looks exactly like the number 8 lying down. Imagine that covered with ice and snow and you have Dorje Lakpa.

Guru Padma Sambhava in
Thyangboche Monastery.

The Dorje, Vajra or Sacred Thunderbolt at Swayambhunath.

Dorje Lakpa looms over Bhaktapur.

The Dorje Lakpa you see is described as '... a fierce ice-hung tooth which appears to offer no simple — or safe — line to the summit,' by photographer - mountaineer John Cleare.

There is a fascinating myth connected with Dorje Lakpa and it goes back to the eighth century and the miracle worker Padma Sambhava. Padma Sambhava was born in a lotus in Western India. He travelled to Tibet, Bhutan and Nepal upon the back of a flying tiger — the first ever mountain flight!

He brought with him potent magic and a will to convert the warrior clans of Tibet to Buddhism. Padma Sambhava had to fight evil, but in vanquishing it, he did not kill the evildoers — he turned them Buddhist with his magic.

One demon whom he made Buddhist was Dorje Lekpa who became a Padma Sambhava follower.

Dorje Lekpa is depicted astride a snow lion and he brings protection wherever he goes. He is thought, along with his four brothers, to safeguard the Himalaya from southern intrusions. And many are those who believe he lives on Dorje Lakpa where the ages have brought about a slight name change from Lekpa to Lakpa.

Whether the origins and name of the mountain date

back to a sacred thunderbolt or to a demon who was transformed into a protective deity, Dorje Lakpa wasn't climbed until 1981 despite the fact that it was placed on the 'permitted' list in 1964.

Perhaps the 'ice-hung tooth' was truly difficult to early attempts. The first successful ascent was on October 18, 1981, when a Japanese expedition put four Japanese climbers — Kazunari Murakand, Eeichi Shinyogi, Kunio Kataoka and Makoto Anba — on the summit along with Pemba Tshering Sherpa who, as we have seen, was born on a Saturday!

You can see the fang that is Dorje Lakpa from the high places in Kathmandu Valley and it always reminds me of the demon-turned-protector who rides a snow lion and who is fat and fearsome.

**The peacock feather Phurbi in a
Sacred Vessel or a Phurba.**

PHURBI-GHYACHU

21,840 feet/6,660 metres

Phurbi-Ghyachu dominates the Kathmandu Valley. The rounded humps on either side of a dominant rounded peak rise well above the valley wall and from my special perch atop the Everest Hotel, the restaurant Sherpaland, it feels as though the mountain is a reach of fingers away.

Gorging myself on the view, I once ventured to tell a lady mountaineer that I thought the mountain was specially beautiful.

She agreed but added that its mere 6,660 metres or 21,840 feet made it unremarkable, unmemorable, and unworthy of more than mere passing comment. How the Himalaya spoil one. On any other continent, Phurbi-Ghyachu would have a queue waiting to climb it.

Phurbi-Ghyachu is a name associated with Buddhist religious rituals and the oceanic beginnings of the Himalaya.

On religious occasions, Lamas carry with them a vessel full of holy water which is sprinkled on people with a peacock feather dipped in the vessel. Together the container and the feather are as familiar to Buddhism as a prayer wheel or a sacred scarf.

The feather that is carried upright inside the vessel is called a Phurbi — that which blesses.

Sherpas believe that the mountain looks like a peacock feather held in a pot full of sacred water.

Ghyachu means ocean.

Put together, Phurbi-Ghyachu means 'The Peacock Feather that Rises from the Ocean'.

The ocean is an obvious reference to the Sea of Tethys that was dissipated when India collided with Eurasia 65 million years ago.

So in calling the mountain Phurbi-Ghyachu, Sherpas recall the sea that was and the sacred peacock feather which blesses living things.

Phurbi-Ghyachu was climbed by the Japanese climber, Ichiro Yasuda, in 1982, and he put 16 people on top of the summit on May 1 and May 3.

It is generally believed in Nepali circles that after World War II the Japanese needed to rebuild morale in their war-torn country. So, as the country healed its many wounds, many high publicity expeditions to the Himalaya were undertaken. Soon it became a national habit and mountain after mountain was scaled by Japanese teams.

Watching Phurbi-Ghyachu catch fire at sunset and turn from yellow to pink to blue above the darkness of the valley, is to believe in peacock feathers and vanished

Phurbi-Ghyachu from the roof of the
Everest Hotel

oceans and the creation of Mother Earth who allows such wonders to happen at the close of every winter's day. Summers are spent waiting for Phurbi-Ghyachu to reappear.

A detail of Chobas or Tormas.

CHOBA-BHAMARE

19,282 feet/5,933 metres

"**N**o peak surpassed for sharpness—," says Tom Weir in his book, *East of Kathmandu.*

"... a conspicuous rock tower ... visible from Kathmandu where it is known as Jobo Bhamare, the identity of this superb feature is confusing: Schneider labels it Chaduk Bhir. A tantalising challenge anyway," writes John Cleare in the *Collins Guide to Mountains and Mountaineering.*

We've always known it as Choba-Bhamare and why Schneider called it Chaduk Bhir and why Cleare calls it Jobo Bhamare must await investigation.

Why it's called Choba-Bhamare is interesting. In monasteries, on special occasions, Lamas make wheat-and-water-paste shapes that are considered sacred, as offerings to the gods. Larger than leaves but often shaped like them, these offerings are about nine to twelve inches high and are sometimes decorated with a mixture of clarified butter and vermilion.

These shapes, these votive offerings to the gods, are called 'tormas' or 'chobas' and a particular prayer might call for as few as two or as many as a hundred of them.

After the prayer, a little is eaten and the rest put at crossroads as a symbolic gesture to invoke beneficial auguries for meetings to come.

Chobas or Tormas offered to
Guru Padma Sambhava in Lukla Monastery.

Choba-Bhamare.

Choba-Bhamare, sticking up like a thumb, looks like one of these votive offerings.

Whereas 'choba' is what the shapes are called, 'bhamare' suggests circular.

So Choba-Bhamare is a circular votive offering to the gods. And so powerful is it that the mountain, though clearly seen, has never been climbed. It remains a tantalising challenge.

Gauri-Shankar

GAURI-SHANKAR

23,185 feet/7,134 metres

t's crowded at the top of Gauri-Shankar.

The Hindu Goddess and God, Gauri and Shankar, live there and Buddhism's Tashi Tsheringma is found on the top of the mountain too. Forunately for both religions, Gauri-Shankar has two peaks.

Tashi Tsheringma is one of the five sisters and is responsible for giving long life to mortals. Miyo Lungsangma, the giver of food, lives on Everest. And so, scattered through the Himalaya are the other three, each with a distinct boon to offer. Tekar Dosangma dispenses good fortune, Chopen Dinsangma blesses with wealth and Thingri Shelsangma gifts telepathic powers. Long life, food, good fortune, wealth and telepathy are the boons offered but the chief function of the goddesses is to protect Buddhism.

Tibetans who fled Tibet through the Himalaya to the south and who have been successful in life, attribute their success to the five goddesses they passed on their way to their new lives. These Tibetans are still Buddhist and though Buddhism might flounder in Tibet it flourishes through Tibetan émigrés in Nepal and India. The five sisters have been successful in a peculiar kind of way.

But the mountain is called Gauri-Shankar and it is this

Tsheringma who lives on Gauri-Shankar.

celestial couple sacred to the Hindus who have guarded the peak fiercely.

Shankar is the holy ascetic form of Shiva. He is perpetually meditating. To ask a boon of him is to receive it at once, as he is said to be impatient to get back to his trance-like state of bliss. Given his way, he'd never surface from his blissful stupor.

But he is not allowed his way.

Gauri, his consort, keeps him from levitating away in a dream-like state. Gauri is Shankar's power and without her he would be the immortal equivalent of dead.

You never ever say "Shankar-Gauri" as you would say "Shiva-Parvati". You always, but always, speak of Gauri-Shankar in that order. The power comes before the glory.

Entire books are written about the exploits of the heavenly ascetic of the Himalaya — Shiva-Shankar. My favourite story is the one in which he was disturbed in his meditation by a demon who, after praying for thousands of years, asked, as a boon, the ability to demolish anyone by merely placing his hand over the victim's head. The boon was granted by a meditation-rapt Shiva-Shankar.

Predictably, the first person the demon wanted to try his new-found powers on was the God Himself.

Shiva-Shankar went to Vishnu, the Preserver of Life, and sought his help. The boon earned by prayer could not be taken back. Shiva-Shankar was in danger of annihilation.

Vishnu transformed himself into a beautiful woman and enticed the demon to dally with her. When the demon was sufficiently besotted, the beautiful woman asked him not to believe in Shiva-Shankar, who was after all a hermit, a dreamer, a mere mendicant. "Why," said the beautiful woman, "he can't give you anything. The boon he granted was nothing. If you don't believe me put your hand over your head."

The demon put his hand over his own head and met instant extinction.

As Shankar, Shiva had to depend on other gods until Gauri came along.

Gauri looks after Shankar now.

I was told of a poem that I have never found, about Gauri-Shankar on their mountain-top, he meditating and she keeping a vigilant eye open for strangers.

Gauri sees a group of men toiling up towards the spot where she and Shankar sit.

"My Lord," says Gauri, "an expedition of mountaineers approaches."

Shankar, incensed, thunders, "How dare they come

Gauri-Shankar from a Nepal Airways flight.

anywhere near me! With a flick of my fingers, I shall send an avalanche to destroy them."

Gauri placates him, "Let them come up a little further. I want to see the colour of the leader's eyes. He is so handsome."

The expedition labours higher and Shankar is indignant, "They're disturbing my calm. I will blow on them and mighty winds will sweep them away."

And Gauri says, "Just a little further. Let them come up. I cannot see the colour of his eyes yet."

As the expedition reaches the final stretch, Gauri says, "He is so handsome. His eyes are blue. Now, my Lord, do as you will."

The climbers die.

Raymond Lambert, leader of an unsuccessful expedition, declared the mountain unclimbable above 18,000 feet. This was in the fifties.

Then in 1964, Don Whillan's British team were forced down by an avalanche which attacked them at 22,000 feet.

Until 1977 no further expeditions were permitted.

In 1979, an American-Nepali party led by Al Reed and Pertemba Sherpa put John Roskelley and Dorje Sherpa on the summit on May 8.

The gods were kind that day.

MELUNGTSE

22,824 feet/7,023 metres

elungtse could mean the 'Fire Wind Peak', and in naming it, the Sherpas went against geology and hearkened back to a time when the mountain may have been volcanic and the spouting fires of the mountain were tamed and extinguished by high winds.

Or Melungtse could mean the 'Strange and Lonely Peak'. For Sherpas, a place where they do not know people and from where the friendly customs they follow are absent, is called 'Melung' which means 'strange and lonely'. I have heard Kathmandu and Pokhara described as 'Melung' by Sherpas going to these towns for the first time.

'Tse' means peak.

Melungtse is strange and lonely because it is in Tibet, its beautiful starkness adding to its alienation for Sherpas.

The Chinese name is 'Qiao Ge Ru' and resembles the Tibetan one 'Jobo Garu'.

'Jobo' could well be an appellation of the word 'Choba', which besides being a votive offering is also the flowing garment that Sherpas and Tibetans wear. To look at, Melungtse does resemble a man's shoulders with a white mantle of cloth drifting downwards. The eastern formation of Melungtse seemingly confirms the humanness of the mountain by looking like a right arm stretched out, the palm placed on a comfortable place miles away, the elbow a hump.

'Ga' means a boundary traditionally made of rocks and boulders. 'Ru' are avalanches. Choba Garu could well imply the Tibetan garment protected by a boundary of boulders and subject to avalanches.

Eric Shipton, who ventured to Melungtse in 1951, said it was an isolated mountain that rose from a glacier basin and added that "on every side its colossal granite walls were pale and smooth as polished marble".

While crossing back into Nepal, the party was stopped and almost arrested by Tibetans. Their good fortune lay in the fact that cupidity triumphed over caution — the Tibetans were bribed.

It is said that quiet expeditions climbed Melungtse in the 50s. But they go unsung.

Then in 1984, Chris Bonington, the British climbing genius, obtained permission from the Chinese authorities to climb Melungtse.

His expedition was met by electrical storms which struck down a member of the team while high winds blew tents to shreds.

It was the weather that forced them to retreat. Bonington

Melungtse from a Necon Air flight.

tried again in 1988 but Melungtse repulsed the team once more.

Then in 1992, on October 23, Slovins, Marko Prezeli and Andrej Stremfelj climbed Melungtse for the first time. Officially.

Time, and the fact that no less a climbing luminary than Chris Bonington himself could not climb Melungtse, will have more expeditions trying for a mountain that has gained the reputation of being difficult.

I am told that sunsets set the peak ablaze just before the cold winds of a Tibetan night are felt by both the mountain and observers. I wonder if that is the fire and the wind that have earned Melungtse its Sherpa name. It seems, less far-fetched geologically and so much more romantic.

CHUGIMAGO

20,465 feet/6,297 metres

dwin Bernbaum, while speaking of unclimbed, unknown peaks, has talked of a dark side to ourselves when we relate to mountains. "The unknown also possesses a darker, more dangerous side; instead of our salvation, it may hold our damnation. The person who ventures into an unexplored range or tries to climb an unclimbed peak, always harbours some fear that instead of what he seeks, he will find disaster and death. Even the hiker, who goes into mountains that others know well, may feel a trace of apprehension. What he finds there in the unknown may shatter his illusions and the comfortable world they uphold. Driven beyond the limits of physical endurance, he may discover things about himself, weaknesses and fears, that he would rather not know." Chugimago rises in a wild, deserted, glacial valley in Southern Rolwaling. Here snow and ice abound and the Himalaya seems to be working hard to earn its 'Abode of Snow' name.

Despite its comparatively low summit at just over 6000 metres, Chugimago has not been climbed. There was a Dutch-German attempt in 1972 but it was not successful.

Since then Chugimago has either not been attempted or no record has been kept of attempts.

Even the name Chugimago suggests a raw, primordial state. The name means 'Peak that Tops Gut Waters'

Apparently, Sherpas see frozen intestinal waters in the glaciers and on the sides of the mountains.

Etched by a series of convoluted, frozen and messy zig-zags, only the pointed, sky thrusting peak or 'Go' has elegance.

So Chugimago awaits climbing, virgin for the moment.

Chugimago from Chola Pass.

PIGFERAGO

21,515 feet/6,620 metres

n naming the mountain 'Ferago' or 'Pherago', the Sherpas hark back to the time when the Himalaya was formed by the collision of two continents. The name means 'Earth Movement Forms Peak'.

The people of Rolwaling where Pigferago is located say that 'Pig' is derived from the English 'Peak'.

In 1960 a French expedition climbed Pigferago but the mountain is off limits now. And Rolwaling too is restricted sometimes, depending apparently on whether 'the hander-out-of-permits' is going by the spirit or the letter of the current law.

Pigferago borders the Khumbu into which the intrepid go via the dreaded Tashi Lapcha Pass.

The Tashi Lapcha always reminds me of Bhanu Bannerjee, who went on expedition with Sir Edmund Hillary. Until then, Bhanu was a nice Bengali boy from Calcutta whose knowledge of height was restricted to the view of that city's 19th century commemorative tower — the Ochterlony Monument.

When Bhanu Bannerjee saw the glacier pass of Tashi Lapcha that is crossed at a height of 5,750 metres / 18,865 feet, he refused to climb it.

From his medical kit, Ed Hillary produced a large blue pill called 'Oblivion' and once he'd swallowed it, a euphoric

Bhanu Bannerjee was willing to float up the Tashi Lapcha.

Until, halfway up, Bhanu Bannerjee went blind. Ed gentled Bhanu down a thousand feet or so and after the snow blindness disappeared, Bhanu overcame his fears and crossed the Tashi Lapcha.

Ed is down for saying that the Tashi Lapcha is one of the more difficult passes encountered in his career as a mountaineer. It was the first high place that Bhanu Bannerjee overcame in his life as a climber.

Pigferago from Chola Pass.

NUMBUR

22,607 feet/6,956 metres

From the gem-like monastery of Chiwang, Numbur is just a flick of the eyes away, and during the celebration of the Mani Rimdu festival, the mountains provide a theatrical backdrop as masked monks in colourful costumes, representing the Buddhist gods triumphing over the Old Bon religion, twirl and leap.

Numbur was probably named by the Sherpas of Solu whose valleys were dominated by this mountain. They were proud of Numbur in the old days. Today's Sherpas, the young bucks, tend to snigger and nudge each other when Numbur is mentioned.

Numbur means the 'Breast'.

And the fine cone of Numbur, imagined by today's youth to belong to a beautiful Sherpa girl, has more celestial connotations for the olden Sherpas of Solu who named it. The mountain is the eternal milk-giver, the mother in the sky who provides sustenance to her Solu children.

Influenced as the Solu Sherpas are by Hinduism and the not-quite-dead Bon of their ancestors — a form of animism — milk is seen as an important and pure form of nourishment.

For Hindus, milk is a votive offering to the gods and is particularly beloved of Shiva and Parvati. And it is milk that is balm to Jupiter and Venus when they agitate mankind with inauspicious astrological influences. Milk is manna for all religious occasions and the only time it is not advised is at the start of journeys. Yoghurt is taken instead.

Cows, as milk givers, are worshipped as mothers in Nepal. Until recently, to kill a cow, even by accident, was to be charged automatically with manslaughter. This was not a whim or fancy. It was the law.

At the base of Numbur is a lake called Dudh Kund which is fed by the waters of the mountain. Dudh Kund means 'lake of milk' and once a year, during the monsoons, a festival celebrating its sacred waters takes place.

Amongst the crowds that throng Dudh Kund are Jhakaris or witch doctors who drink the lake's water and anoint their heads with it. For them, the water, and the mountain that provides it, are sacred and a source of power.

Jhakaris assume that all illness is caused by evil, malign spirits and these primitive, powerful witch doctors are seen to be supreme exorcists. Their secret rituals are passed by oral tradition from father to son, the latter often being an adopted one to keep the art alive.

As a mountain to be climbed, Numbur is a kindly entity

Numbur from Khomjungri.

who allows a high rate of success. The first to reach its summit were Sherpa Mingma Tshering and Japanese climber, Hiroshi Matsuo in the spring of 1963.

I wonder if Mingma Tshering was suitably awed by the summit of Numbur. Or did he snigger his way up every crevice, cranny and niche?

KARYOLUNG

21,160 feet/6,511 metres

ou can see Karyolung as a hovering presence from Lukla where Rik A.D. Sherpa was born and where I was stranded once. The airstrip in Lukla has made the sleepy little village into a bustling town. Lukla is the gateway to Khumbu since Sir Edmund Hillary located and designed the Lukla airstrip.

I was in Lukla helping Desmond Doig design a Sherpa hotel which we decided to call a Sherpatel and the hospitality received by guests was dubbed Sherpatality.

We got stuck there because the weather closed in and along with us, stranded, was a strange collection of people. There was a coffee magnate, a Nepali poet, a western horror-story writer, a conservationist, a future President of the Nepal Mountaineering Association — Dawa Sherpa, and a future Vice-President of the Shangrila Hotel — Utpal Sengupta.

While Utpal and Dawa hunted for fresh mountain goat, the Nepali poet and I talked of high mountains and lost love. The Nepali poet had a girlfriend who lived beneath Karyolung and he was on his way back from an unsuccessful attempt to look for her. He'd written a poem which I helped him to translate and I've kept it for 14 years.

"I couldn't hold you
Because your father
In the mountains
Below Karyolung
Called.

So I wait
In a suddenly
Unenchanted valley
Counting on small planes
To take you letters
Or bring you back.

Your father's tears
In the mountain
Below Karyolung

Are more important
Than my momentary madness
In a suddenly
Unenchanted valley."

That is the only poem that Karyolung has ever inspired. But for the duration of my stay in Lukla, Karyolung became a very personal symbol to me of the mountains beyond, those that I would never walk to.

Karyolung means 'White Place' and though I sound like a detergent advertisement, a whiter whiteness I have never seen. It snowed on Karyolung every night and in the

Karyolag.

Swayambhunath like Boudhnath the
Buddhist shrine has 13 circles that
lead to enlightenment.

mornings the mountain glinted in the sun.

It looks benevolent. But it has repulsed climbers all the way up to the autumn of 1982 when a Japanese expedition led by Yoshiyuki Inove put seven Japanese and six Sherpas on the summit on October 31 and November 1.

The peak of Karyolung has always reminded me of the finial or steeple of Boudhnath. There are 13 gilded rungs that lead to a sharp point on top of the stupa or shrine of Boudhnath. The lowest rung is the widest, like the base of Karyolung. Successive rungs get smaller until you reach the point. So too, as you get higher on Karyolung the mountain becomes sharper.

The 13 rungs on Boudhnath stand for the 13 obstacles that come between man and Nirvana or eternal peace.

The widest rungs at the bottom of the finial symbolise desire, dishonesty and anger. As you conquer these you ascend closer to enlightenment and perpetual bliss.

On Karyolung several expeditions didn't get past the lower, broader base. And I like to think that, however momentarily, Yoshiyuki Inove and his party found tranquillity on the top of Karyolung.

CHO-OYU

26,653 feet/8,201 metres

t is believed that Padma Sambhava, the Lotus-born saint of Buddhism, buried or hid treasures in special places. Not ordinary treasures that mean material wealth, but spiritual ones.

Foreseeing a time when religion would mean nothing, when laws would be broken, when lamas would be disobeyed and when even the gods would hear of earth's chaos, Padma Sambhava wrote sacred texts that would be Man's salvation. These books are the treasures. In Tibet, Padma Sambhava or Guru Rimpoche as he is also called, saw war and the flight of people. So the books, these sacred texts, were hidden on Tibet's border.

The sacred texts of the lamas are called Cho. Yu is the Sherpa word for turquoise. The mountain Cho-Oyu could be 'Place of the Turquoise Text'.

The accepted interpretation of Cho-Oyu is 'Goddess of the Turquoise'.

Whichever is correct, the important word is 'turquoise'.

Sherpas love turquoise.

A favourite story tells of a Sherpa who was travelling by horseback when a female Yeti, abominable snow woman, stopped him. Like all good Sherpas, this one believed that the end had come, as Yetis eat Sherpas.

The Lady Yeti took the Sherpa to a cave where her family

Cho Oyo from Gokyo.

was. The Sherpa was now convinced he was going to be the family's main course for the day.

But the Yeti showed him her child who was choking on something. She asked the Sherpa to help. The Sherpa thumped the small Yeti on the back, dislodging a human, presumably Sherpa, bone. The little Yeti breathed freely again.

Besides not eating the Sherpa, a gift of eight bound bags were given to him as doctor's fee. But instructions were also given to him to open the bags only in a secret place.

In seclusion at home, the Sherpa opened his gifts.

Eight female heads spilled out.

Each hair on each head held a turquoise. The Sherpa, rich now for several generations, named himself Yuthok Sherpa.

Near Cho-Oyu is the Nangpa-la, the pass into Tibet — all passes are called 'la'— which Yuthok traversed to go into that country to bring back turquoise and salt.

It was from the Nagpa-la that the 1921 Everest Reconnaissance Expedition, exploring the world's highest peak from the Tibetan side, saw and photographed Cho-Oyu.

In 1951 Shipton's Everest Reconnaissance said of Cho-Oyu that there was 'not one chink in its icy armour'.

In 1952, while seven Englishmen and three New Zealanders trained with Shipton for an Everest attempt, they tried Cho-Oyu in May. They got to over 6,000 metres but couldn't get past the ice cliffs there because they were not properly equipped. One of the New Zealanders was a young man named Edmund Hillary.

Cho-Oyu was finally climbed in 1954 by an Austrian expedition led by Tichy.

Cho-Oyu is considered the easiest 8,000-metre mountain and some 400 people have been on its summit. But lives have been lost too. Claude Kogan, the famous lady climber, was killed as were skiers Huber and Thurmayer.

Easy is definitely a comparative word in the Himalaya.

GYACHUNG KANG

25,844 feet/7,952 metres

"Difficult. Steep and straight up," said a mountain archivist while describing Gyachung Kang. She may well have been illustrating life.

Like the steeples of cathedrals, the spires of temples and multi-tiered heights of pagoda-roofed shrines, the mountains have been used as a metaphor for a bridge between a troublesome life and a tranquil heaven.

But the worship-places of man are built by man and the mountains were created by nature—or by the gods. Man climbs mountains to gain summits which are a step towards heaven. Climbing is a sport with serious intent, howsoever subconscious that intent may be.

And a journey up a mountain is often a journey of self discovery. At the end of the Hindu epic, the *Mahabharata*, the five brothers, who are central to the epic, labour up a mythical Himalayan mountain, Meru.

One by one they fall victim to their own weaknesses that are revealed as they toil up the high mountain. Gluttony, pride and other fallibilities of the human condition devastate the band of travellers until only the purest, Yudhishthir, who refuses to let his brothers face damnation or to leave his faithful dog, survives the journey.

He alone, in a divine, free-of-imperfection form, enters heaven, is reunited with his family and is placed beyond suffering and sorrow.

If life is a mountain climb, then he who receives a mountain like Gyachung Kang as a journey to salvation is unlucky indeed.

Gyachung Kang, which means the 'Mountain that Rose from the Great Sea that Was', reminding us once more of the vanished Sea of Tethys, is a formidable ascent.

On April 10 and 11, 1960, five Japanese and Sherpa Pasang Phutar III attained the summit. The expedition leader was Kazuyoshi Kohara. There have been only two successful teams since.

There will be others. Defeat invites renewed attempts. Some will succeed. Some will not. Some will experience the exhilaration of a 'job' well done, others will experience dejection. Hopefully only a very few, if any, will die.

And Ghyachung Kang's analogy to the circle of life and the business of living will complete itself again and again.

Gyachung Kang from Gokyo Peak

PUMORI

23,292 feet/7,161 metres

In 1761 Jean Jacques Rousseau published a novel, *La Nouvelle Heloise*, and with that book, the novelist-philosopher influenced poets, mountaineers and lay people to look anew at mountains as a source that offered physical well-being and a rejuvenation of the spirit.

Upon climbing a minor peak in the Alps, the hero of the novel, Sainte-Preux observes, "It was there that I visibly discerned, in the purity of the air in which I found myself, the true cause of the change in my mood, and the return of the inner peace that I had lost for so long. In effect, it is a general impression experienced by all men, even though they do not all observe it, that on high mountains, where the air is pure and subtle, one feels greater ease in breathing, more lightness in the body, greater serenity in the spirit; pleasures are less ardent there, passions more moderate. Meditations take on inexpressibly grand and sublime character in proportion to the objects that impress us, a tranquil voluptuousness that has nothing to do with anyting harsh or sensual. It seems that in rising above the dwellings of men, one leaves behind all low and earthly sentiments, and to the degree that one approaches the ethereal regions, the soul acquires something of their unalterable purity."

The paragraph and the book had people thronging to

the Alps. It influenced a whole generation of English poets and eventually it helped to popularise mountaineering as not just a physical sport but one endowed with the spiritual.

It was from a background where mountains called for the total commitment of body, mind and soul, that the 'Sir Galahad of Climbing', George Mallory, came to meet the Himalaya.

He was determined to climb Everest.

While expeditioning in the Himalaya, Mallory gave an unnamed mountain the name 'Pumori' or 'Daughter Peak' after his daughter Clare.

Pumori was first attempted in 1953 by John Cunningham and Hamish Mac Innes, but they were beaten back by avalanches and bad weather.

In 1953, an Indian expedition, too, failed.

In 1961, a three-man German-Swiss expedition led by Gert Mehl unofficially tried to climb the mountain while filming a documentary, *The Sherpa as Porter and Climber.* They failed. Then in April 1962, a German-Swiss expedition led by Gerhard Lanser ascended Pumori. Ascended, not conquered.

In the early Himalayan years the word 'conquest' was often used to describe the successful ascent of a

Pumori from Kala Pathar.

mountain. But a quote from Mallory in the 20s reappeared and put an end to words that suggested conquering. "Have we vanquished an enemy? None but ourselves."

Nuptse from Kala Pathar.

NUPTSE

25,528 feet/7,855 metres

herpas doomed Nuptse to be considered subsidiary by simply calling it Nuptse. Nuptse means 'West Peak', because the mountain is to the west of Everest. To Sherpas, as to everybody else in the world, Everest comes first, Everest is the centre, the focal point. All else comes second. Including Nuptse.

The ascent of Nuptse is difficult. Despite several attempts, only two expeditions to date have reached the mountain's highest summit.

But the more difficult a mountain, the more prized it becomes.

One of the earliest literary climbers was Dante. In his *Divine Comedy* with the poet Virgil acting as his guide, Dante climbs Mount Purgatory. It too is a difficult mountain. At first.

As he ascends, Dante sees souls ridding themselves of the Seven Deadly Sins.

The most difficult sin to overcome is pride which is the lowest terrace. To overcome pride, a soul must accept its own inadequacy and turn to God's grace to achieve fulfilment. In casting away the 'I' and depending only on the 'Thou', lies the way to the next terrace, envy. And so the Soul goes, expunging wrath, slothfulness, greed, gluttony and last of all, lust.

And then the summit is achieved.

Virgil explains this to Dante, "The mountain is such that even at the beginning below, it is toilsome, but the higher one goes, the less one wearies. Therefore, when it shall seem to you so pleasant that the going up is as easy for you as going downstream in a boat, then will you be at the end of the path : hope there to rest your weariness..."

But Nuptse, more hell than purgatory, was difficult throughout for Chris Bonington's British party in 1961. Finally at 4.00 p.m. on May 16 and again on May 17, four Englishmen and two Sherpas reached the summit.

In 1975, following the same route, a British-Nepali attempt met with disaster: three members and a Sherpa died.

Dante and Virgil would conclude that each of us must seek individual ways to attain the earthly paradise atop our own Mount Purgatory.

EVEREST
SAGARMATHA
CHOMOLUNGMA

29,028 feet/8,848 metres

The young man could barely contain his excitement as he was ushered into the presence of his superior. He wanted to be calm and collected. But he found himself blurting it all out at once. "Sir, I've discovered the highest mountain in the world." And so Radhanath Sikdar made his one entry into history.

Sikdar was an Indian surveyor who was measuring mountains from the State of Bihar in India and had come upon the highest mountain in the world in nearby —but closed — Nepal.

His ultimate superior was Andrew Waugh, Surveyor General of the Great Trigonometrical Survey of India, a man who suspected that there was a mountain higher than the known Kanchenjunga.

Waugh is believed to have glimpsed this mountain and one of his staff called it 'B'. It was he who had sent Sikdar and others to find and measure it.

The year was 1849.

Waugh had teams at work for the next three years, and in 1852 Roman numerals were given to this extraordinarily high peak. It was called Peak XV.

In naming it, a process that took years, Andrew Waugh ignored the fact that the Tibetans had a name for it and set about trying to call it Everest, after his predecessor

George Everest, who he felt was deserving of the honour. Waugh wrote, "... in testimony of my affectionate respect for a revered chief, and to perpetuate the memory of that illustrious master of accurate geographical research...."

There was one tiny matter that stood between Waugh and naming the mountain Everest.

George Everest himself.

The man who had pioneered new and more precise ways of measuring mountains was wary of honours and, more strongly, George Everest was of the firm opinion that Himalayan peaks should wear their original names.

George Everest declared that the name Everest could not be pronounced by 'the natives of India' nor could it be written in Hindi.

That the great geographer made no mention of Nepal, could be owing to the fact that he was not allowed into the country in 1840 when he sought permission and, therefore, had no idea what it was like.

By 1865, a year before he died, George Everest relented. Peak XV became Everest and Everest became a household word.

Chomolungma was the name Tibet knew the mountain by. And records show that in 650 AD, early Tibetan kings had birds fed at their expense in an area around a high mountain known as Lhochamalung or the 'Place Where Birds Are Kept'.

In 1733, French cartographer d'Anville published a map with the name Tschoumou Lanckma meaning 'Goddess Mother of the World'.

Actually the mountain had over 50 variations of the name, my favourite being the 'Mountain Over Which No Birds Fly'.

Chomolungma is being used more often now by classicists. And one of the interpretations which is gaining credence today is that the Tibetan name is an application of the name Miyolangsangma, the 'Goddess of Long Life', who is said to live on the mountain.

Miyolangsangma is depicted as a golden goddess riding a tiger and holding a bowl of roasted flour, accompanied by a jewel-spitting mongoose.

At Thyangboche monastery, which many say was 'built in contemplation of the highest peak', a yak is set free during the dance festival of Mani Rimdu. The yak becomes a ward of Miyolangsangma and is free to wander the mountains.

When Nepal learned it had the highest mountain in the world, officials worked out the name Sagarmatha — 'One Whose Forehead Reaches Up to the Sky'.

Miyolangangma who lives on Everest.

Sagarmatha, too, has mythological echoes. After Vishnu had drunk dry the Sea of Tethys, the Divine Protector rested, leaving the newly created Mother Earth alone and unprotected.

A demon attacked Mother Earth and parts of her body were spread all over the globe. Her limbs became the Himalaya and it could be her forehead that touches the sky.

Several expeditions attempted Everest from the Tibetan side, the most famous of which may well have actually climbed the mountain. It was the 1924 expedition of British climbers.

The expedition had on it the 'Sir Galahad of Mountaineering,' George Mallory, who found a partner in 22-year-old Andrew Irvine because the latter was enthusiastic and could deal with the heavy oxygen apparatus they had to carry.

Climbing in support of Mallory and Irvine was Noel Odell, who on June 8, 1924, wrote: "The entire Summit Ridge and final peak of Everest were unveiled. My eyes became fixed on one tiny black spot silhouetted on a small snow-crest beneath a rock step in the ridge; the black spot moved. Another black spot became apparent and moved up the snow to join the other on the crest. The first then approached the great Rock Step and shortly emerged at the top; the second did likewise.

Then the whole fascinating vision vanished, enveloped in cloud once more."

The spots were Mallory and Irvine.

Mallory and Irvine were never seen again. The riddle that puzzles the mountaineering world to this day is whether, being so close to the top, Irvine and Mallory had actually climbed the mountain before they disappeared.

There are reasons for belief in the '24 ascent of Everest.

In a little known book, *Why I Believe in Personal Immortality* by the late Sir Oliver Lodge, the author writes of a communication received by the spirit of Frederic Myers on September 14, 1924. The message was that Irvine and Mallory had reached the peak of Mount Everest and having planted a flag, were on their way down when they died. Their bodies were to be found lying frozen on a ledge a hundred feet down.

Then, in the book, Irvine himself is said to have sent another other-worldly communication to his friend Arnold Lunn in which the mountaineer revealed that his body would be found crouching under a shelf of rock and that in the left hand inside pocket of his coat were papers in which he had entered his last record: "Summit reached, flag planted, food giving out, we begin to descend."

Everest from Kala Pathar.

But there are many more reasons to disbelieve in Mallory and Irvine's ascent of the summit.

Between the 1924 expedition and proven success in 1953 there were at least 10 parties that attempted Everest and failed.

Finally, in 1953, a British expedition led by Col H.C.J. Hunt, comprising 14 members, attempted Everest. The expedition was like a military assault. Even so, the first summit team failed.

Then on May 29, Hillary and Sherpa Tenzing attained the world's highest summit.

It was Tenzing's seventh expedition to the mountain.

The ascent coincided with Queen Elizabeth's coronation. A new era had begun.

On the back of the book *Everest* edited by Peter Gillman is a blurb that says, ". . . 40 years that saw a total of 485 ascents by 13 different routes."

It is not my intention to go more deeply into the climbing of Everest. But there are some notable climbs that might be of interest.

1975, first ascent by a woman, Mrs Junko Tabei, from Japan.

1978, first ascent without oxygen, Reinhold Messner, Peter Habeler.

1980, first solo ascent by Reinhold Messner.

1985, Dick Bass becomes the oldest man up Everest at 55 and completes all seven top summits of the world's continents.

1988, Marc Batard solos Everest in $22^1/_2$ hours.

1990, Bertand 'Zebulon' Roche from France becomes the youngest Everest summiteer at 17.

1990, a Joint Peace expedition comprising members from U.S.A., U.S.S.R. and China puts 20 on to Everest.

1993, Ramon Blance Suarez aged 60 replaces Dick Bass as the oldest man to climb Everest.

Besides being climbed, Everest has been skied down, and ballooned over but the fascination of the mountain remains.

But beyond the firsts, the records and the statistics, lies a mountain. Everest, Chomolungma, Sagarmatha: call it what you will, it brings out the best in men and women. It brings out the spirit of adventure that longs for unreachable stars.

Why do people climb Everest? Why do people climb a mountain? The best answer ever given was by George Mallory. "Because it's there," he said. What remained unsaid was that because it's there, it's a challenge and where there's challenge, Man appears and surmounts. Ultimately.

Lhotse from Dingboche.

LHOTSE

27,677 feet/8,516 metres

hotse means 'South Peak' and the mountain is located to the south of Everest, which most people, especially Sherpas, have regarded as the tall centre of the peaks it dominates.

Lhotse is the eastern part of the Nuptse-Lhotse wall, from behind which Everest peers out towards the south.

It's these environs that abound in lore about the Yeti.

The Tibetans call the Yeti 'mi-gyu', which roughly translates to 'being of the nature of man'. But wrongly translated — as it was by an early British columnist — it means 'the abominable snowman'.

Respectable explorers such as Colonel C.K. Howard-Bury saw strangely human but enormous footprints in the snow in 1921 while leading an Everest Reconnaissance Expedition. It was, incidentally, Howard-Bury who wrote about 'a huge amphitheatre of mighty peaks culminating in a new and unsurveyed peak, 28,100 ft in height, to which we gave the name Lhotse, which in Tibetan means the 'South Peak'.

So in one expedition Howard-Bury meets the footprint of Yeti and names a mountain.

In fact there were so many Yeti and Yeti-footprint sightings that Sir Edmund Hillary led an expedition to look for it.

On the expedition was Desmond Doig.

After much searching they found nothing, but they did take the famous 'Yeti scalp' from Khumjung monastery to Chicago, Paris and London where it was declared an artifact, a man-made item fashioned from the hide of a wild Himalayan goat.

Sir Edmund was satisfied that the Yeti was a creature of the imagination.

Desmond Doig was convinced it existed.

Why else, reasoned Desmond, would people in Bhutan, Nepal and Sikkim describe exactly the same kind of creature; people, he argued, who had never met each other?

In Bhutan, it is believed that to see a Yeti, one has to dress and smell like a Yak herdsman, then Yetis are likely to come out to greet one.

In Sikkim, a royal personage during the first half of the century described the Yeti to perfection and insisted that the creature came to tea — in a pith helmet!

And in Nepal, around Lhotse, people say many Yetis would be seen were it not for the famous picnic.

Yetis menaced the monks of a monastery to such an extent that it was decided that, however colourful, the animals must go.

So a picnic was planned.

Out in the open, the monks drank a little rice wine, ate a little rice and then fell upon each other with wooden swords and knives.

The hidden Yetis watched.

The monks put out poisoned rice and wine and real knives before retreating into their monastery.

At night, the Yetis emerged.

Being natural mimics, they ate and drank the tainted food and wine and then killed each other with the wickedly sharp knives. Desmond Doig believed that the Yeti was the Himalayan Blue Bear that normally walked on all fours but was given to standing on its hind legs and moving at great speed.

Blue Bear or some other enormous hairy creature lurks around the mountains near Lhotse, waiting to be found. Or so Desmond used to think.

And why not?

After all, it was Howard-Bury who, as recently as 1921, 'discovered' and named Lhotse and that was an 8000-metre peak, not a mere man-sized Yeti.

The first ascent of Lhotse came over thirty years later, in 1956, when Luchsinger and Reiss of the Swiss Expedition reached the peak on May 18.

Nine expeditions later, in 1977, came the second, third and fourth ascents by a 13-member German expedition led by Schmatz. He put nine people on the summit.

There have been many expeditions to Lhotse and whether they succeeded or failed, they proved a point. Lhotse is a mountain in its own right and not just an extension of Everest. And like all mountains, it is worthy of respect.

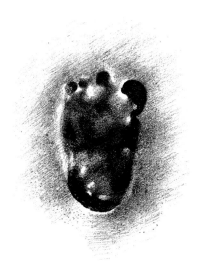

A Dablam, carries the image of a God or saint.

AMA DABLAM

22,139 feet/6,812 metres

t's a beautiful, wonderful mountain. Just like the mountains children sketch. You can see it from almost everywhere in Sherpa country. And Sherpas call it Ama Dablam— 'Mother's Amulet for Deities'.

The amulet is worn on a necklace or on a belt at the side, near the waist. It is a series of three arches, the topmost one forming a peak. Just like the mountain.

It was climbed in 1961 by Mike Gill, Barry Bishop, Mike Ward and Wally Romaines on March 13.

They were members of Sir Edmund Hillary's 'Himalayan Scientific and Mountaineering Expedition'. They hunted the Yeti, climbed Ama Dablam and spent a winter at high altitude on the mountain's flank in a silver hut.

Rockets were being invented and shot into space in those early days and one of the missions of the expedition was to find out how man would react to high altitudes over a long period of time.

Desmond Doig was on the expedition and used to talk of the dreadful effects. He used to say you slowed down and didn't know you were slowing down. Your speech was slow, your movements slowed and your mind objected to even comparatively fast moving things.

After being in the hut for weeks, Desmond found that

people fresh from the outside were moving too fast, speaking too loudly and speedily. It was only afterwards that he realised it was he who had slowed down.

When the expedition got back to Kathmandu, it was in time for Queen Elizabeth's visit to Nepal. The British Ambassador to the country was going to be knighted. Everyone, including the Hillary team, was asked to a party.

It was a garden party. And there was a cake. It was huge, brown, white, and at the top it had two marzipan figures of Tenzing and Hillary stuck near the summit. People who were there at the time recall it being a dreadful cake.

The mountaineers, Ed Hillary included, hovered at the edge of the gathering.

Her Majesty the Queen was given a ceremonial sword to cut the cake.

She raised the sword.

Then looking over at the expedition, she said, "Ah, Sir Edmund, I fear I shall have to cut you in half!" Also present at the party was Khunjo Chumbi, the village elder from Sherpa country, his wife and newborn baby. Mrs Chumbi had delivered the child at a lunch break during the 14-day walk between her village and Kathmandu so as not to delay her husband's march to the capital. He had to be present at the request and requirement of Her Brittanic Majesty.

Khunjo Chumbi had accompanied Ed Hillary and Desmond to America, England and France as guardian of the Yeti scalp. In London he had left gifts of tea, cheese and Yak tails for the Queen at Buckingham Palace. The Queen wanted to say 'thank you' in person while in Kathmandu.

The Chumbis had bought Sherpa outfits for both the Queen and Prince Philip.

In the rooms at the embassy, while they tried on their Sherpa finery Prince Philip asked the age of the infant Mrs Chumbi carried.

Mrs Chumbi said he was only a few days old.

Did he have a name, questioned Prince Philip.

And when Mrs Chumbi said 'no' the Prince said, "Call him Philip. I'll be his Godfather."

Philip Chumbi works at a trekking agency in Kathmandu but at the family shrine in the mountains are pictures of himself, his mother and father and Prince Philip.

Khunjo Chumbi died recently but his house in Khumjung still overlooks his favourite mountain — Ama Dablam.

Ama Dablam from Thyangboche.

Chamlang.

CHAMLANG

23,786 feet/7,319 metres

"**C**hamlang. It's a lovely mountain," said Dr. Gil Roberts. "It's a mini Kanchenjunga with its ridge of peaks."

For me, Gil, the mountaineering doctor, is a poet of the mountains. Just to spend time with him is to have the mountains come alive.

"Each mountain has a persona that is distinct and individual. Climbing mountains is a sort of metaphor for life but there are no lies or half truths or evasions on a mountain. You either do something or you don't." As Gil talked, up on the seventh floor of the Everest Hotel, the afternoon turned golden and the mountains that stretch out to forever were bathed in light.

Gil is a director of the American Himalayan Foundation and his wife, Erica Stone, is Executive Director.

Together they voice the needs of mountain people and help to raise funds to see those needs met. Sir Edmund Hillary's Himalayan Trust and the American Himalayan Foundation do more for mountains than more august, better funded bodies do.

Gil was on the 1963 Everest expedition and was on a rope with a friend who was killed by an avalanche as they climbed together. Gil had to do that most impossible of things — cut the rope.

Gil has stopped climbing but he and Erica come out

once a year to the Nepal Himalaya to see how they can help the people and the environment.

Chamlang translates as the 'Sacred Dance of the Ox'. And the mountain does look like an ox with its head at the western end and a sloping back that trails off towards the east.

But why a sacred dance?

Erica has seen Tibetans do a timeless yak dance and it could be argued that it had its beginnings in religion.

A more pragmatic view states that the Sherpas who named the mountain were drunk at the time and for them all 7,319 metres swayed as though dancing.

The highest of Chamlang's summits was climbed in 1962, on May 31, by Soh Anma and Pasang Phutar Sherpa III who were on a Japanese expedition.

For them at least, the ox did not do its celestial dance.

Mahakala in Kathmandu.

MAKALU

27,504 feet/8,463 metres

He is a fierce and fearsome God. Mahakala, the Great Black. In Tibet and Buddhism he is known as Nagpochenpo. In Hinduism, he is Mahakala, God of Death. He is depicted as sitting on corpses.

Mahakala lives in Tibet but flies to Assam in India, his second abode. And his flight takes him over the Himalaya and over one mountain in particular and it bears his name — Makalu.

The story goes that as Mahakala flew over Kathmandu Valley a magician who had great powers saw him and wanted to hold the Lord of Death as Protector of the Valley.

So Jamuna Gubaju, the magician, threw some enchanted grains of rice into the air which struck Mahakala and brought the God to earth.

"Why have you captured me?" thundered Mahakala.

"Because Mankind in the valley needs you," countered Jamuna Gubaju.

"I will not stay," said the God, "but I will visit this place on Saturdays and do for you in that one day what would take me seven in other parts of the world."

The shrine to Mahakala is near the green flatness of Kathmandu's ground-for-all-reasons, the Tundikhel.

Below the shrine is my favourite bookshop, Educational Enterprises.

I have seen the shrine crowded on Saturdays as people offer Mahakala large vessels full of liquor of the most potent kind.

It is believed that death can be foretold by the liquor. If it's spilled, then the sick person on whose behalf it has been offered will die. If the liquor remains in its container, the patient will survive. One's hands have to be steady in the presence of the Great Black One.

There was a king of Kathmandu, once, who had four wives. His favourite, the youngest, got smallpox and was at death's door. The king appealed to all the gods to save her. But the queen died.

In a rage, the king went from temple to temple desecrating the stone, metal or wooden gods. When he came to Mahakala he raised a foot to kick the deity but the carved corpse on which Mahakala stood rolled a full nine feet and stopped the king.

The king began worshipping Mahakala from that day on.

As Nepal was closed to foreigners, in 1934, a French expedition hoping to scale Makalu applied to the Tibetan Government for permission to climb. It was granted, but even as the French prepared for the expedition, a change of decision took place and the permission was cancelled.

Ed Hillary photographed the west face of Makalu in 1951 and was the first to come close to it in 1952, and to attempt to climb it in 1954. He had an accident but continued until he was taken seriously ill. The attempt was abandoned.

A French team led by J. Franco ascended the mountain and teams reached the top in three summit attempts on the May 15, 16 and 17, 1955.

In 1961, Hillary tried Makalu again but was taken ill on the mountain a second time.

Mahakala was obviously trying to convey a message to Sir Edmund Hillary.

Makalu from Dingboche Peak.

Kanchenjunga .

KANCHENJUNGA

27,943 feet/8,598 metres

Kanchenjunga has five summits and the mountain's name is derived from a Tibetan word that means the 'Five Treasures of the Great Snow' or the 'Five Brothers of the Great Snow'. To the Sikkimese there is no place on earth more sacred. The late Sir Tashi Namgyal, the Chogyal or ruler of Sikkim, used to ask mountaineers to leave the summit, at least, unclimbed.

Most mountaineers obliged. Beginning with Charles Evans, who led the 1955 British Kanchenjunga expedition. He declared the mountain climbed when his team was twenty feet away from the top.

Later mountaineers were not as reverent and one particular total ascent of Kanchenjunga is blamed for the annexation of Sikkim by India.

The highest peak of the mountain is said to hide gold, another silver, the third conceals jewels and the fourth contains grain. The last holds the sacred books of Padma Sambhava. These are the 'Five Treasures'.

The 'Five Brothers of the Great Snow' refers to celestial deities mounted on divine carriers such as a winged lion, an other-worldly elephant, a flying horse, a dragon in the clouds and a soaring eagle. The brothers protect the treasures.

The God atop Kanchenjunga is Vaisravana, the God of

Wealth, who rides a snow lion that plays on top of mountains. It is believed that one day, Vaisravana will dispense his treasures when humanity is in need.

In another version of the tale, Kanchenjunga was a warrior god who took his name from the mountain. It is this god, disguised as a white bird, who showed the 17th century Tibetan monk, Lhatsun Chembo, the way into Sikkim. Lhatsun Chembo brought a royal house of Tibetan descent into Sikkim and, through them, converted the animist dwellers of Sikkim, into Buddhists. The Lepchas, the original, pre-Buddhist inhabitants of Sikkim were believers in the forces of nature and they too worshipped Kanchenjunga as a place where the dead go. They called the mountain Konglo Chu, 'The Highest Veil of Ice', and believed that the first man and woman were fashioned from the ice of Kanchenjunga's glaciers.

Both religions celebrate the dance of Kanchenjunga each year on the day that, according to Buddhists, the Bringer of Buddhism, Lhatsun Chembo, came to Sikkim and the day, according to the Lepchas, that Kongchen the deity of Kanchenjunga, has to be appeased.

The dance is started by a whirl of colourful 'warriors' who sanctify the ground before the figure of Kanchenjunga arrives in silks and brocades and wearing a terrifying, protective red mask.

Five flags, symbolising the peaks, flutter from his helmet.

His dance is a slow and stately one and at the culmination, Sikkim is declared safe for yet another year.

The first attempt on Kanchenjunga was in 1905 by a Swiss party which invited A. Crowley, a British climber, to be its leader and took along an Italian hotelier called de Righi, from Darjeeling.

On September 1, two of the Swiss members and de Righi, while coming down the mountain after having reached a high point of 6,500 metres, met with an accident. One of the Swiss mountaineers and three Indians who were helping them were killed; de Righi fainted and was buried in snow. The survivors cried out for help. A Swiss climber went down to see what he could do.

Crowley sat in his tent drinking tea and is recorded as saying, "A mountain accident of this sort is one of the things for which I have no sympathy whatsoever. Tomorrow I hope to go down and find out how things stand."

Crowley thought the surviving Swiss 'old enough to rescue himself, and nobody would want to rescue de Righi.'

Crowley styled himself the Great Beast.

There were several expeditions, but it was the 1955 Evans Expedition that met with success on May 25.

Ed Bernbaum described Kanchenjunga as giving "an overwhelming impression of lightness and grace... presents a vision not so much of a mountain as of another world floating like a cloud above ours".

A ZEN EPILOGUE

There was once a monk who lived high in the mountains. He was poor and had no possessions. He lived on berries and leaves and the sight of the mountains. His being was full of their beauty and through them he acquired wisdom.

One day, a thief came upon the monk and seeing he was poor, apologised for the intrusion and was about to leave when the monk stopped him.

"I have these clothes and you cannot go away empty-handed," said the monk.

And he gave the thief his clothes.

Alone, the monk sat sipping water from an earthen cup when suddenly he saw the reflection of the mountains and the sky and the beauty of his surroundings reflected in the water he was sipping.

"Poor thief," said the monk to himself, "I could not give him this."

To you, who have seen the mountains and have been amongst them, is imparted a richness of spirit. Whatever you felt when you saw the Himalaya is yours and yours alone. You can talk about it a million times and still keep their beautiful shapes and their soundless sound in your mind.

Whatever else you lose in your life, this no one can ever take from you — your memory of mountains.

Brigand's Bend,
Thaguwater-on-Trisuli,
Nepal.
December 1993.

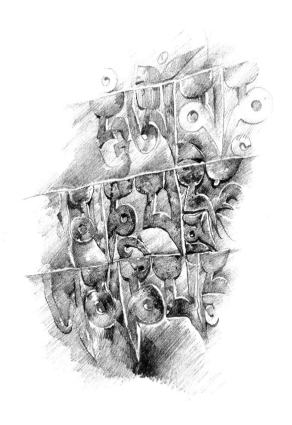

SELECTED BIBLIOGRAPHY

John Clare, *Collins' Guide to Mountains and Mountaineers.*

Edwin Bernbaum, *Sacred Mountains of the World.*

Peter Gillman, *Everest, the Best Writing and Pictures from Seventy Years of Human Endeavour.*

Jill Neate, *High Asia, an Illustrated History of the 7000-metre Peaks.*

Ian Cameron, *Mountains of the Gods: The Himalaya and the Mountains of Central Asia.*

Walt Unsworth, *Encyclopedia of Mountaineering.*

Stan Armington, *Trekking in the Nepal Himalaya.*

Louis C. Baume, *Sivalaya: Exploration of the 8000-metre Peaks of the Himalaya.*

Stephen Bezruchka, *Trekking in Nepal: a Traveller's Guide.*

Rene de Milleville and Trilok C. Majupuria, *Magnificent Nepal Himalaya (in a nutshell).*

Margaret Jefferies, *Sagarmatha: Mother of the Universe,*

The Story of Mt. Everest National Park.

Khempo Sangay Tenzin and Gomehen Oleshey, (Translated by Keith Dowman.), *Deities & Divinities of Tibet (the Nyingma Icons), A Collection of Line Drawings of Deities & Divinities.*

New Larousse Encyclopedia of Mythology.

Lisa Choegyal, *Insight Guides Nepal.*

Marvlin M. Rhie and Robert A. F. Thurman, *The Sacred Art of Tibet.*

Desmond Doig, *My Kind of Kathmandu : An Artist's Impression of the Emerald Valley.*